BULLFIGHTI

JUN 2010

Bullfighting

A troubled history

Elisabeth Hardouin-Fugier

REAKTION BOOKS

For Professor Maurice Agulhon

Published by Reaktion Books Ltd
33 Great Sutton Street
London EC1V 0DX, UK
www.reaktionbooks.co.uk

First published 2010

Copyright © Elisabeth Hardouin-Fugier 2010

Translated from the French by Sue Rose

The publishers gratefully acknowledge support for the publication of this book
by CAS International (Comité Anti Stierenvechten), Utrecht, The Netherlands.

Printed and bound in China
by Toppan Printing Co. Ltd

British Library Cataloguing in Publication Data
Hardouin-Fugier, Elisabeth.
  A history of bullfighting.
  1. Bullfights – History.
  2. Bullfights – Cross-cultural studies.
  3. Bullfights in art.
  4. Bullfights in literature.
  I. Title
  791.8'2'09-DC22

ISBN 978 1 86189 518 9

Contents

Joseph Albers, *Bullfight, San Sebastian*, 1930, photo collage on cardboard.

one

Fighting Bulls

THE CORRIDA

Corrida, the French and Spanish word for a bull-fight, initially referred to some kind of a race between a man and a bull, with either the animal pursuing the man or, conversely, the man chasing the animal. In the bullring, a fast sprinter will race past a bull, plunging in *banderillas* (darts with a barbed harpoon) at top speed, while the matador, on the contrary, endeavours to stand his ground to demonstrate his composure in the face of an attack by a formidable adversary. However, the word *corrida* also still refers to a foot race in Spain and, in the eighteenth century, the Spanish language, as well as the language of the South of France (Langue d'Oc), used to employ the expression *courir les taureaux*, similar to the English term 'bull running', as opposed to *courir après les taureaux* ('running *after* bulls').[1]

Running was almost certainly the first method used by men to catch their prey, and this is reflected in the French term for hunting, *chasse à courre*, which retains the redundant verb *courre* (to run), as well as in the English term for the medieval hunt, known as 'running with hounds'. In these cases, the actual act of running was often enough to kill the animal, which, finally unable to continue, would collapse in exhaustion. When in the mid-nineteenth century the Spanish mode of bullfighting was imported into France, it was named *course de taureaux*, again picking up the idea of running – an inaccurate term when referring to a spectacle held in a bullring that maintained the illusion of a contest between bulls, in which no blood was spilled, much the same as the equestrian sport which, in France, deserves its name of *course de chevaux* (horse-racing). This latter expression, which fell out of use in France around 1920, was the term used by ill-informed French lawyers in 1951, when the so-called Loi Grammont of 2 July 1851 brought bullfighting into the French legal system.[2]

The word *tauromachy* is more general, although it now refers only to the male of the bovine species; in ancient times, *tauromachy* might have been a contest *between* bulls or cows, as in the Canton of Valais in Switzerland where, since 1923, spectators have been able to watch cows engaging in a natural battle to determine the dominant animal in the herd.[3] The English and German equivalents for the word *corrida* are military in nature – bull-baiting, bullfighting and *Stierkampf* – although these terms do not make it clear that the bull is bound to lose. They evoke the European take on war, which requires the enemy to be exterminated, as opposed to the Latin American format, which requires the enemy to be captured alive, his death being

Francisco Goya, *Banderillas with Firecrackers*, 1816, preparatory red chalk drawing for *Tauromaquia*.

Francisco Goya, *The Way in which the Ancient Spaniards Hunted Bulls on Horseback in the Open Country*, 1816, preparatory red chalk drawing for *Tauromaquia*.

Bullfight held in Madrid in Honour of the Infanta, 18th century, etching.

deferred as a sacrificial offering. This difference in the strategies and weapons of war is reflected in the different bullfighting techniques that prevail in Europe and Latin America.

In the nineteenth century a Spanish newspaper, the *Gaceta de Madrid*, described the extravagant nature of the eagerly awaited celebrations of sovereignty held for the populace in Madrid on important occasions. The splendid religious services with huge choirs were followed by artillery salvos and the lavish spectacle of horsemen surrounded by 100 footmen wearing their colours, as well as firework displays, comic theatrical entertainments, masked balls, horseback cane games and, inevitably, the public killing of '14 *toros de muerte*' (bulls that fight to the death) by the noblest knights in the kingdom.[4] Bloodshed formed an integral part of the Spanish celebrations of sovereignty, which appropriated the equestrian rules of hunting and war, and reinforced the aristocratic privileges underpinning the established order. The killing of bulls for

entertainment mimicked an ancient hunt, with lances, in which the horseman aimed at the cerebellum to ensure a rapid kill.

The slaughter of the bull by a horseman armed with a lance recalls the iconography of St George fighting the dragon. Representatives of the civil, political, military and religious orders took part in the ostentatious spectacles staged by the established hierarchies. These festivals referred back to a past event that reinforced the authority of those in power, often a founding myth, like royal birth, canonization or a coronation; these seminal events found expression in the anachronistic weapons and opulent costumes that glittered with gold from the Americas.

The populace would gather along the route taken by the carriages, which were exhibited with all due pomp and circumstance, and watch the displays of bullfighting from a distance. The subjects were given live bulls on which they in turn collectively performed acts of cruelty, often with makeshift weapons like knives, sticks and

José Rubio de Villegas, *Bullfight held on the Plaza Mayor for the Marriage of Isabella II and her Sister with the Duke of Montpensier, Son of the King of France Louis-Philippe, 16 October 1846*, c. 1846, oil on canvas.

pitchforks. A great deal of meat was consumed. Small gifts, coins and sweets, were thrown into the crowd in a jubilant, spendthrift atmosphere. Throughout the Spanish kingdom, the spectacles organized to celebrate sovereignty were essential to the workings of political and religious power but, in the early years, bullfighting merely referred back to the founding treatise written by the creators of the spectacle (1796). Its horses, swords and costumes gave it an aristocratic appearance, but the impetus was the violence of a bloody spectacle.

In South America, the conquistadors held the first bullfights as celebrations of sovereignty to strengthen their authority over the Indians and, more importantly, over their overambitious compatriots. Everything about these events was terrifying. The horses were unfamiliar to the

Indians; according to one witness, Stanislas Arlet, the Indians believed horse and rider to be one creature.[5] The bulls, which were also imported, quickly proliferated, damaging pasture-lands, ravaging native food crops and overrunning the cities. The sword, which had never been seen before by Indians, appeared to be an extension of the arm and hand. Last, the deadly imports also included explosives. During the conquest of South America, the significance of these weapons, particularly the sword, was 'that one culture uses violence to deny another and, by denying it, ensures that the only value left is

death'.[6] In fact, the conquistadors' bullfights in the sixteenth century took place at the same time as a genocide that wiped out 'an entire people to such an extent that its memory of its own civilization was erased'.[7]

BULL GAMES

'Bull games' were festive entertainments that brought together spectators and participants in an event that tended to charge an admission fee, although it could sometimes be free. In mass public events, the spectators also took part, con-fronting a bull that sometimes emerged unhurt

The Pamplona bull-run in the 1920s.

Philips Galle, 'Bullfight', from the series *Hunting Parties*, *c.* 1578, engraving.

from the spectacle, as in the Spanish *encierros* or *abrivados* (bull-running events). Men would bait, overtake or pursue the bull in these events, which mimicked the simple, utilitarian moving of herds from one place to another. In Pamplona, the bulls earmarked for the *corrida* were released into the streets, and participants had nothing to gain except glory and the pleasure of taking part. In the current French *Courses Camarguaises,* the objective is to grab the rosettes attached between the horns of various bulls in a closed arena watched by spectators. Unless there is an accident, no blood is spilled, and the bull is just another participant. However, the symbolic prize can sometimes be valuable. In Cuzco (Peru), coins and silver stars are either stuck onto the bull's hide or attached to strips of metal embedded in the animal's flesh. In many places in Latin America, lottery tickets, or splendid embroidered fabrics called *enjalmas*, tied onto the bull with straps or ribbons, are so highly coveted that they can lead to fighting between competitors and occasionally to the death of the animal, which becomes more of a target than a participant in the game.

As soon as the maltreatment of animals became a factor, the 'game' aspect disappeared in favour of the notion of combat. Most 'bull games' included some kind of arms drill that was not always lethal: the Portuguese-style bullfight was restricted to the use of *banderillas*. A euphemistic vocabulary – 'baiting', 'teasing' – masked the gory reality of a spectacle in which suffering became the driving force and the animal became the victim. Publically torturing an animal that has been reared for that purpose raises questions. Cruelty to animals is 'an assertion of social superiority . . . Many of the poor saw the gentry's dogs, horses and deer as symbols of aristocratic privilege . . . to be callously mutilated in some defiant gesture of social protest'.[8] This is an expression of the principle 'I suffer, therefore I inflict pain', the perfect motto for sadists. Sociological analysis has demonstrated that cruel village festivals were the launch pad for bullfighting, which was then appropriated by the political world with its financial considerations, wars and machismo.[9] Contrary to rumour, festive violence against domestic animals does not appear to be directly related to the practice of breeding. Both Brazil and Argentina, which are centres for international breeding, banned bullfighting.

The *capeas* were theoretically bullfights in which only lures were used. They were held in specially adapted village squares in both France and Spain until the early twentieth century, when they were banned. The participants waved lures, such as pieces of fabric, cowherd's capes or hats in front of the bulls, trying to make them catch the fabric on their horns. Young men, eager to attract female admiration, waved capes to provoke cowardly bulls in temporary enclosures, formed by carts and wooden fences. Only some of the cattle reacted to this stratagem, which was used by cowherds to move herds from one place to another. Some of the passes caused the animal to fall or move unnaturally and, for this reason, were liable to cause injury. The *capeas* were dangerous for the participants, because the bulls that had been previously used in them became 'wise' to the use of lures, and aimed for the men, not the fabric.

RURAL FESTIVALS

Cruel rural festivals are still organized in many places in Spain, drawing fans who have sometimes travelled across Europe, as well as people opposed to these spectacles. The maltreatment of bulls in festivals has been and is still so

Bull-baiting in Germany, late 17th century.

widespread in Spain that it has given rise to a specific vocabulary. *Toros ensogados* or *enmaromados* were roped by the horns, particularly during fights between animals. In one painting, the Venetian painter, Gabriele Bella, depicted a roped bull attacked by various animals, decapitated birds, dogs fighting a bear, and a cat hanging by the belly. In London and Paris, popular engravings show dogs or bears, sometimes leashed, attacking a bull at the end of a rope. *Toros de cohete* or *encohetes* were covered with fireworks, which set alight the animal's back. *Toros de fuego* had balls of combustible materials attached to their horns.

Vargas Ponce was a horrified witness to various cruel village festivals.[10] In 1807, this navigator and renowned topographer gave a report to the Academy in Madrid on the subject of bullfighting and other cruel festivals. He listed the tortures in order of the natural elements, water, air and fire: bulls were tormented in water until they drowned, others were hurled from the tops of cliffs (or now, from bell-towers), *toros precipitados*. There was a particular fascination with fire in Latin America: covered in gunpowder, their horns surrounded by oakum soaked in inflammable products, the *toros enmantados* became living torches, *toros encandellados*; these were practices that had originated in times of war and were suspected to be used by arsonists. Vargas Ponce itemized the types of suffering endured by the animal, using some emotive terms: 'martyrdom', 'torture', 'innocent victim', 'tormented', 'poor bull', 'despair'. He stigmatized men who *hieren, pinchan, apalean* (hurt, prick, beat); the torturers exhibited an 'exquisite bloodthirstiness and barbarity' that far exceeded those of the animal. Thirteen of the 34 engraved plates in the first edition of Goya's *Tauromaquia* carried texts inspired by Vargas

Eugenio Lucas Velàzquez (1817–70), *Bullfight*, oil on canvas.

Attrib. Francisco Goya, *Bullfight in a Divided Ring*, c. 1800–29, oil on canvas.

Ignacio Zuloaga (1870–1945), *A Bullfight in my Village*, oil on canvas.

Ponce.[11] Some of the plates show festive acts of cruelty that Goya attributed to archaic men, sometimes Moors, when they were actually being performed during his lifetime (and are even still carried out today) in village festivals. For example, he depicted men armed with lances impaling a bull, as people once did and continue to do at the Toro de la Vega.

THE BULLRING

Fighting in the bullring was a more technical event than the festivals since it created an innovative succession of weapons whose effects were skilfully calculated. The three fundamental weapons used in bullfighting were the lance, the *banderillas* and the sword. In addition to these weapons were the ranch colours, attached to a lance planted behind the bull's shoulder blade, and the *banderillas* of fire, which had firecrackers attached to their shafts that exploded when embedded in the animal's flesh. The disembowelling of the horse by the bull recreated a fight between animals, taken to its limits in the Andes where, incredibly, on occasion a live condor, its wings held by at least four men, has its talons sewn tightly into the bull's *morillo* (the hump of muscle at the base of the bull's neck) using an awl threaded with string. The more recent *descabello* is a straight sword with a crosspiece near the end of the blade, resembling a cross between a sword and a dagger or *puntilla*. The picador's iron stirrups caused injury; the sharp point of the stick in the *muleta* (red flannel cloth) could be used discreetly to jab at the eyes and muzzle. The *estocada a recibir* (death blow given with the *estoque* sword) used the momentum from the bull's charge to impale the animal, various knives and pincers gashed the flesh and pulled out the *banderillas*, often while the animal

Francisco Goya, *Banderillas de Fuego*, detail from a print in the *Tauromaquia* series.

was still alive, and a knife was used to cut off the ear, then the medulla oblongata (the lower portion of the brainstem). The bullfighting techniques were also weapons in their own right, such as the cape passes that caused anatomical injury to the bull and the practice of twisting the animal's tail, then standing on it to crush it against the ground and prevent the animal from getting up. In Latin America they used lassos, firecrackers attached to the animal or fireworks, as well as the Indian club. One of the attractions of the burgeoning bullfight was to add a good ten weapons, which were for the most part known to

An 18th-century ink-and-wash drawing of the placing of the *banderillas* by a matador.

could entertain guests and show off their financial status. In Lima (Peru), everything ground to a halt in the town on bullfight days. The *toril* (bullpen) was filled from nightfall: 'the rabble . . . infuriated the bulls . . . by poking their nostrils' and pricking them. From dawn, 'the rabble stormed the gates . . . in the midst of an intense excitement which nothing could equal.'[12] The crowd swarmed into the bullring, emptied by the soldiers for the bullfight. Countless food vendors walked around crying their various wares. Spectators brought in and purchased a large quantity of strong spirits, and ate their meals during the spectacle. The 'din [is] incredible, the people . . . speak excitedly, shout, sing, call to each other from one terrace to another, argue, and resort to blows to settle their quarrels.' In Spain, men and women were allowed to sit together in the bullring, which was not the case in the theatre. The author of the pamphlet attributed to Jovellanos[13] described the atmosphere: 'there the pressure, noise, heat, and dust, joined to the aromatic sweets of tobacco, wine and garlic, are sufficient to cause suffocation . . . a most fruitful seminary for diseases.' A proverb confirmed 'If you go to the *toros*, it will cost you two reales and a raging fever.'[14]

The bullring was said to be an animated scene 'where luxury, profligacy, shamelessness, libertinism, stupidity and, in short, every vice which disgraces human nature hold their court'. Women came alone to prostitute themselves. The event gave priests an excuse 'for spending amongst sinners the price of their sins', it gave magistrates 'the sure means of destroying all idea of civil liberty', and tradesmen the 'consolation of beholding the death of animals which, if living, would find them constant employment'. The nobles were 'eager to patronize these barbarous spectacles; to honour

the spectators and used by them in their villages, whether Indian, Spanish or French. At the bullfight, the villagers were on familiar territory.

The colourful crowds that took their seats in the new bullrings, often for the whole day and part of the night, entered a closed world, one that resembled a journey into the unknown. The price of the seats, ranging from 2 to 220 *reales*, kept the social classes separate. The most expensive place to sit was in the boxes, which were as luxurious as little apartments, where spectators

TAUREAU. — *Courses de taureaux* : 1. Le taureau ; 2. L'espada ; 3. Banderillero ; 4. Chulo ; 5. Picador ; 6. Muletier ; 7. Chef de quadrille provençale ; 8. Ecarteur landais ; 9. Défilé de la quadrille ; 10. L'alguazil apportant la clef du toril ; 11. Jeu du picador ; 12. Jeu du chulo ; 13. Jeu du banderillero ; 14. Jeu de l'espada : mort du taureau ; 15. Les mules enlevant le taureau tué ; 16. Course landaise ; 17. Conducteur de troupeau (*vaquero*) ; 18. Conduite d'un troupeau.

Illustrations for the article 'Taureau' in the *Dictionnaire Larousse Illustré* (1910).

the bull-fighters . . . and to vie with each other, in protecting the most villainous characters in the republic'.[15] Travellers told of a surprising habituation to the cruelty of the spectacle, which they had not expected in women.

A representative of the authorities was in charge of the event, supported by soldiers or police officers. The crowd communicated with him by shouting – for example, demanding that they bring in the dogs to tear the bull from limb to limb. Later, the use of colour-coded hand-kerchiefs was introduced as a mode of communication. As a way of maintaining interest, a bull was sometimes 'given over to the pleasure of the people, who descended into the bullring to fight'; they vied with each other to beat it to death.[16]

ANDALUCIA

Bullfighting is to Seville what the gondola is to Venice. The Andalusians took the cowherd's cape pass, deployed to usher cattle from one place to another, and devised a technique that combined an effective procedure with an almost chorographic set of movements to prepare for the bull's death from the moment the animal entered the ring. Its repeated charges to follow the lure began a process of deoxygenation that did not impair its healthy appearance. The passes were codified, specialized, named and therefore easily identifiable. Although other bullfighting centres like Pamplona made their mark early, it did not take long for the Andalusians to realize that, for a skill to be evaluated, it had to be measured

Antonio Carnicero, Bullfighter talking to a picador on horseback, from a *Collection of the Main Actions in a Bullfight*, 1780s, hand-coloured etching.

against known, fixed rules, hence the need for the spectacle to be codified as though it were a sport.[17] Around 80 per cent of the matadors in Spain before 1830 were Andalusian.

The abattoirs in the San Bernardo district of Seville met the increased demand for meat. If the animal died a slow death, this was supposed to improve the meat. 'A good butcher bleeds an animal for a long time, at least eight to ten minutes.' Some stabbed the animal with a knife and came back the next day to collect it when it was dead. Some slaughterers 'amused themselves' by injuring the bulls before they were slaughtered. Spectators wanting to enjoy this free entertainment would climb on the roofs, damaging them in the process, hence the municipal ban on this type of practice in 1601. An engraving by Joris Hoefnagel depicts a view of Seville in the late sixteenth century: men armed with lances appear to be fighting a bull in front of the abattoir. Ronda, in eastern Andalucia, was also a breeding ground for renowned matadors and the birthplace of the Romero family, the alleged inventors of the *estocada a volapié* (when the matador runs towards the bull), which is the centrepiece of a bullfight. Various Andalusians made names for themselves as matadors, such as 'Costillares' (Joaquín Rodríguez, 1743–1800) and 'Pepe-Hillo' (José Delgado Guerra, 1754–1801), who, in 1796, published the most important practical treatise on bullfighting, his *Tratado de Tauromaquia*.[18]

The fame of Andalusian bullfighting also owed a great deal to Seville's prestige, despite the transfer in 1717 of the Casa de Contratación (the office handling exports to South America) to Cadiz and the waning importance of its inland port, which became silted up and so overtaken by coastal Cadiz. In Seville, the new-style bullfight nurtured a thriving tourist industry. Under Charles III (r. 1759–1788), during a general economic revival, manufacturing activity picked up in Andalusia and the matadors showcased Andalusian silk in the bullring with their capes. The persona of Carmen promoted manufactured tobacco (1757), which was smoked on the terraces in cigars or rolled up in a piece of paper, much to the astonishment of travellers. The powder stores supplied explosives for the *banderillas de castigo* (punishment spears). The matadors' swords came from Toledo. The bulls were also Andalusian, although they were rivalled by ranches in Aranjuez from 1740. The Court's sojourn in Seville was beneficial to the bullring (rebuilt in 1734), which staged the first performances by the riders from what is now the 'Royal' Maestranza de Caballería, followed soon afterwards by the first bullfights.

MAKING THE MATADOR

Tauromachy or the art of bullfighting was included in military manuals as part of a soldier's training, and bullfights were commonly held during fiestas. In 17th-century Spain, horsemanship was the prerogative of aristocratic warriors, whose mounts had to know how to sidestep the enemy on the battlefield. In the seventeenth century, the lances of old were replaced by the *rejón*, a short javelin with a long hook that was driven into the bull's back by the horsemen as they rode past. The mounted bullfighters were accompanied by men on foot wearing their colours and carrying their swords. Mounted bullfighting with the *rejón* developed into a spectacle, sometimes with an admission charge, that was held on specially adapted squares or in one of the very few bullrings that existed at that time. The Plaza de la Maestranza in Seville

'Episodes from a Bullfight', a collection of *Images populaires rouges*.

(a cavalry armoury) was frequently hired out and brought in an annual revenue of 100,000 *reales*. Around 1740 a Swiss painter described and illustrated a mounted bullfight;[19] it did not take long to kill the bull by aiming the *rejón* at the base of its head. The bullring depicted could be that of Soto de Luzon in Madrid, for which there are accounts dating back to 1737. In Diderot's famous *Encyclopédie*, an article describes the bull being killed by the men on foot, who are assisting an unhorsed bullfighter: 'sword in hand [a member of the team] cuts off one of the bull's legs with a single stroke'. The bullfighters 'cut and thrust' at the bull.[20]

However, around the middle of the century, the aristocracy began to lose interest in the waning art of horsemanship. A new breed of bullfighters performing on foot breathed fresh life into the spectacle. This represented an added value to bull meat. A succession of bladed weapons inflicted different wounds on the bull; the lance proddings incited the animal to disembowel the horse. This spectacular goring became the *corrida*'s loss leader. Killing the bull with a sword marked the *torero*'s (bullfighter's) apotheosis. The bull's slow death on the ground owed much to the horrors of eighteenth-century abattoirs.

Anatomical science had clarified the role of the lungs in the circulatory system, and these organs were punctured by the sword during the bullfight to cause non-visible internal haemorrhaging, thereby avoiding any resemblance to the bleeding of meat for alimentary purposes.[21] Theatrical devices started being used in the arena: the bullfighters wielded swords and were attired

Juan de la Cruz, *The Famous Pedro Romero*, c. 1770s–80s, coloured etching.

Antonio Carnicero, a *torero* preparing to stab a bull, from a *Collection of the Main Actions in a Bullfight*, 1780s, hand-coloured etching.

Entrada de la cuadrilla.

Suerte de Vara

Quite de caballo

Banderillas

Pase de Muleta

El Arrastre

in brightly coloured costumes. A menacing bull thundered into the ring, confronting a weak-looking adversary who, turning the tables, killed the bull and emerged the victor. The hero, with whom the spectators identified, claimed to be 'superior . . . even to the laws of society and nature', in other words, to death.

The new Bourbon king of Spain, Philip V (r. 1700–1740), had no great liking for the bull-fights that were regularly staged on his journey from the Pyrenean border to Madrid, as if to familiarize him with the Spanish *corrida*. This new type of spectacle was just one of the many changes taking place in the Western world:[22] migration to the cities had led to a decline in

farming, and the flourishing urban bourgeoisie was hungry for entertainment and consumable goods, like meat, which held a position of growing importance. A new type of capitalism was taking hold, linked to market expansion in Latin America and a trade that was causing an increase in the number of middlemen – cattle traders, carriers and so on.

THE *TERCIOS*

The First Tercio or act which began the bullfight was the Tercio de Varas, which could be called the 'blood and guts' act, since it involved the use of lances and the goring of horses. When the bull entered the bullring, looking to all intents and

What the bull sees at the gate into the ring at Alès (Gard, France).

6 CORRIDA DE TOROS — Le Taureau enlève
le Picador et son Cheval. RM

A bull tossing the picador and his horse. The horse is unprotected.

purposes unharmed (in fact, it had sometimes been sedated and had its horns shortened), the matador's assistants (*peons*), wearing lavish costumes decorated with gleaming braid, attracted the animal by making various passes with capes, both to tire it and, more importantly, to put its temperament to the test. The bull was wounded initially with a shafted weapon. In its pasture, the bull rarely attacked the herdsmen's horses but, in the bullring, the terrified bull resorted to its natural form of defence, fleeing. The picador then attempted to wound the bull to make it attack the horse. In his treatise on bullfighting, *Tauromaquia*, Pepe-Hillo claimed to be infuriated at the ignorance of riders who were incapable of avoiding the charging bull, which plunged its horns into the horse's belly and unhorsed the rider. In the opinion of Emmanuel Witz, skilled riders used to make a deal with the organizers to pay for the dead horses but, because of the numbers involved, the latter would buy cheap horses bound for the knackers' yards, 'invalid workers from mills and factories, agricultural horses, cab horses, all weary with long years of hard work . . . unhappy outcasts who were to be sweated up to the last moment of their lives'.[23] They were also sold by the army's cavalry, which at that time maintained 6,000 head of horses. This gave rise, perhaps involuntarily, to the best loss leader of the *corrida*, the goring of horses in

An injured horse being lifted.

the bullring, which would send spectators into a frenzy. The *Diario de Madrid* reported that in five seasons of bullfighting (1790 to 1795), over 1,500 horses had been killed or at least disembowelled. In fact, horses that could still stand were packed with straw or sawdust and stitched up again on the spot, so they could be reused.[24] Around two bulls out of three killed a horse. Spectators at a bullfight in the late eighteenth century had a good chance of seeing between three (4 November 1793) and 28 (14 May 1792) horses killed. From 1790 to 1795, between 180 and 191 horses were killed in the ring each season.[25]

In the eighteenth century, the picador's lance or *pica* was mainly used to incite the bull to charge and the spectacle resembled an animated battlefield, where the matador's assistants made passes with their capes to lead the bulls away from the unhorsed riders. The bulls received many shallow wounds from the lance. The *pica* developed over the years, acquiring a pyramid-shaped tip with razor-sharp edges. The rope-covered ball that was theoretically supposed to restrict the depth of penetration of the point was replaced by a small bar. However, in Mexico, this was often made of plastic and the picador could always open the bull's hide with the tip to drive the blade, and even part of the shaft, into the gash. The account of a surgical operation, under anaesthetic, to save a bull that had fought and been spared (1995, Mexico), provides accurate information about this practice. The veterinary surgeon refers to a 30-centimetre-deep hole made by a *pica*, and a sword wound in which the vet was able to 'insert his hand up to the elbow'.[26] The time-honoured use of the *pica* was to tear the *morillo*, a mound of muscle on the bull's back, which caused the animal to lower its head and made it easier to deal the death blow. For many years, countless photographs, corroborated by the testimony of bull-fighting fans, have shown *picas* positioned in the middle of the bull's back. The *pica* could therefore break the spine, the lumbar vertebrae or the ribs, or even perforate the pleura and hinder breathing, or damage the nerves of the spinal column, causing paralysis. The picador, obeying the orders of the matador, more or less crippled the bull without the spectators' knowledge.

José Gutiérrez Solana, *The Bullring*, 1923, oil on canvas.

Caparisoned horse, picador and *cuadrilla* in the bullring.

In the Second Tercio, *banderillas* decorated with ribbons were placed at high speed, as though at the beginning of a hunt; but in the *corrida*, this Tercio was the central act. The harpoon on the end of the *banderilla* was razor sharp and had an 'anti-reverse' barb, like a fish hook, that prevented the blade (about 4 cm long) from working free of the wound. The design of the point has barely changed since then. Pictures by Goya show Moors placing long-handled harpoons. After a handle put out a matador's eye, the handles were made to be jointed, so they hung downwards. The *banderillero* placed it on the run, usually moving in the opposite direction to the bull. This excellent sprinter held the *banderillas* with his arms raised, then plunged them in near the *morillo* with each

hand, making good use of his momentum. Three pairs of *banderillas* were used in Europe while five pairs were common in the top Mexican bull-rings. The swinging handles caused the points to tear the flesh. During the above-mentioned operation of 1995, the veterinary surgeon removed the *banderillas* and explored their trajectory with forceps. He removed fragments of wood, paper, sand, hairs, steel wire and necrosed skin from these wounds.[27] In the bullring, pincers and knives were used to remove the *banderillas* from bulls that had collapsed on the ground but were often still alive; their eyes blinked and quivered, as could be seen in a film by Pablo Knudsen.[28] The coloured paper decoration was reminiscent of the feather fletching on arrows and javelins and served as festive emblems. In Venezuela, flowers were added, from which ring-doves escaped.[29] The text for a poster for the Whitsun Feria in Nîmes (May 1994), centred on brightly-coloured paper, read: *'Feria de Pentecôte, dense, colorée, musicale'* (Whitsun Feria, crowded, colourful, musical).

The *banderillas de castigo*, known as 'punishment spears', which were also called 'widows' because of their black paper decoration, were used on bulls that, true to nature, attempted to escape. They were called *manso* (cowardly) and were 'punished'. The 16-cm blade embedded a gunpowder charge in the wound, where it exploded. In his *Tauromaquia*, Goya depicted the *banderillero* being handed some smoking *banderillas*. After several fruitless bans (1854), they were abolished by Alphonse XII around 1901 but, due to their popularity in Latin America, they continued to be used in Mexico City.

If the bull kept trying to escape, the crowd would shout for the dogs, crying *Peros*! *'Messieurs les chiens'*, as described by Théophile Gautier, were abattoir watchdogs, like Berganza, the dog whom Cervantes made his mouthpiece.[30] Berganza boasted about easily mastering this technique at the abattoir in Seville, outside one of the city gates, the Puerto do la Carne. In England, a special breed of dog, the bulldog, was used by butchers to antagonize the bulls before they were slaughtered in order to improve the meat. This became an established practice in some countries, although it was prohibited in others. English travellers to Spain recognized the spectacle of 'bull-baiting', which was heartily enjoyed in England; there the bull was usually tethered and sometimes pitted against bears, and often abattoir watchdogs.[31] Several travellers described this practice in a Spanish bullring: 'and at length a great bull-dog was let loose at him . . . Another dog was then set at him, and he remained without defence. He still dragged the dogs along, but the latter kept their hold, and continued to hang by his ears. To separate them, eight very

Injuries caused by the lance, the *divisa* (red ribbon) and *banderillas*.

strong men advanced into the arena, seized the bull by the tail to deprive him of the use of his strength, then took him by the hindfeet, threw him down and pinched him in a tender part. Thus he lay quite faint and lifeless, and the dogs immediately quitted their hold . . . the same scene (was) renewed six or seven times successively'.[32]

In the Third Tercio, the bull was stabbed beyond recovery. The fastest way to kill an immobilized bull was to slit its throat by severing the large blood vessels in the neck, thereby causing massive blood loss. This process, which was deemed contemptible, was not allowed in a bullfight. The noble weapon, the sword, was used to bring the spectacle to a theatrical close. This required a costly apprenticeship and the courage to get close to the enemy, which was not the case with firearms, which were also viewed with contempt. From the art of fencing, the *corrida* borrowed its gliding steps, the legendary 'equality

of opportunity' of duelling with swords and the term 'the hour of truth'. The theatrical effect of the process was skilfully described by Théophile Gautier: 'A silvery flash passed with the rapidity of lightening between the two crescents, and the bull fell upon his knees with a roar of pain. He had got the hilt of the sword between his shoulders'.[33] The invention of the *estocada* (circa 1730), which appears to have replaced the massive sword thrust that broke the second cervical vertebra and sliced through the spinal cord,[34] was attributed by Pepe-Hillo to Francisco Romero. Romero's *estocada* was subtle, if risky. The blade has to enter an area measuring only a few centimetres, called *la cruz* (the cross, on the animal's right-hand side), then travel behind the shoulder blade, entering the fourth intercostal space and ending up in the lung. The internal haemorrhage caused by severing the pulmonary or cardiac blood vessels often leaves the animal standing

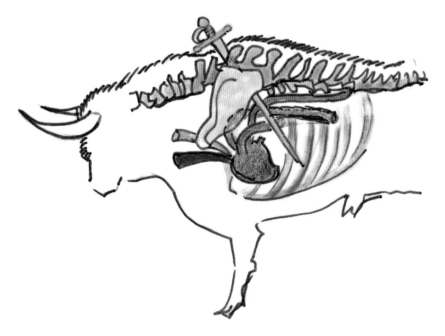

Trajectory of the sword through the rib-cage. The heart and posterior aorta are shown in red.

Francisco Goya, 'They loose dogs on the bull', plate 25 from *Tauromaquia*, 1816, engraving.

long enough to guarantee a dramatic effect. This raises the question as to whether the matador who performs the *estocada* is a butcher or a skilled anatomist.

In order to execute this complicated thrust successfully, the matador must contort his body: he 'crosses' himself by carrying out several simultaneous moves in opposite directions. He has to keep the animal's head tilted downwards by waving the *muleta* (cloth mounted on a horizontal shaft) with his left hand but on his right-hand side; then raise the sword horizontally with his right hand, to plunge it *'en la cruz'*. This last move requires the matador to perform the impressive feat of leaning over the bull very close to the right horn (called *perfilar*, 'profiling'). The *estocada* is a skilful manoeuvre that relies heavily on luck, since the sword may strike bone. A good many calves obviously have to be slaughtered before the matador can learn to perform this flamboyant move successfully. The blow rarely causes the bull to drop to the ground, so the matador has to plunge the sword in, then pull it out. The massive suffering caused by the *estocada* in a bullfight is purely for theatrical effect. Furthermore, the *estocada* is rarely a death blow. If, fortunately, the bull drops immediately (a 'conclusive *estocada*'), it is due to exhaustion and asphyxiation; having lost a great deal of blood and used up all its oxygen running, the bull ends up suffocating because its lungs are flooded. If the bull remains on its feet, the matador tries decerebration (striking the base of the medulla oblongata) with a special sword, the *descabello*. This blow often fails: it took the famous Dominguín as many as 30 blows to fell the bull with the *descabello*. All that is important for the spectacle is that the bull drops to the ground.

The bull's agonizing death throes on the ground formed the Fourth Tercio. According to the rules, the animal now belonged to the butcher, not the matador. *Aficionados* (fans of bullfighting)

Matador profiling to make the kill.

claim that its suffering could not be imputed to the *corrida*. The cheering crowd awarded the triumphant matador trophies – the ears or tail – which were hastily cut off, often while the downed bull was still alive, because it was almost never dead at this point, as confirmed by the famous matador, Montes, in 1830. Today, many autopsies have confirmed that the *estocada* generally fells the bull, but does not kill it. In 1927, one veterinarian, Pierre Matté,[35] performed an autopsy on 27 bulls killed in French bullrings. A committed *aficionado*, he wrote: 'In most cases, the *puntillero* is the one who [kills] the bull. The *estocada* itself is not enough to kill, delivering the *estocada* with a sword would only

kill after a slow, painful death; so-called conclusive *estocadas* are rarely the true cause of death.' Even better: the matador fells the animal, but it is the *puntillero* who does away with it.

THE ABATTOIR

According to fans of bullfighting, the abattoir was worse than the *corrida* and they believed it was better to 'battle the bull than butcher it'. This verbal sophistry ignored the animal's slow, agonizing death on the ground. The bullfighters stood on the bull's tail to immobilize it, then the *puntillero* attempted to decerebrate it, but this was impossible to do successfully straight away, and the bull could receive as many as 30 blows with the *puntilla*. The members of the bullfighter's team (the *peons*) in the bullring, keen to waste no time in handing the trophies to the matador, who wanted to do his lap of honour, often cut off the animal's ear while it was still alive, then removed the *banderillas* with pincers and knives, while its open eyes flickered. However, in large-scale bullfights, the *peons* tried to hide the scene with their outspread capes. According to many accounts, a large number of living bulls were brought to the *desolladero* or slaughterhouse, where they were hung up while still alive, resulting in dislocated femurs. They only died when they were bled.

The *puntilla* was used in 18th-century abattoirs, when the downed bull was on the ground,[36] to try and sever the base of the medulla oblongata by sliding the blade into the small gap where the upper cervical vertebras join the base of the skull. This process was criticized from the 18th century onwards because it paralyzed the animal without killing it or knocking it out, and it was abandoned in the 19th century. In the 20th century, humanitarian slaughtering recommended the use of the captive bolt pistol, which stunned the animal, and this became the established method used virtually everywhere. However, in Spain a decree passed on 5 December 1918 imposed slaughtering by means of the *puntilla* to the exclusion of all other methods. In 1976, on Franco's death, a decree stated that the *puntilla* was not mandatory, but it was only in the year following Spain's entry into the European Union in 1986 that the use of the *puntilla* in abattoirs was abandoned.[37] However, in 1991 an abattoir employee known as Tobalo was found to be helping *banderilleros* practise with the *puntilla*.[38] So, between 1918 and 1987 millions of Spanish bulls were tortured with the *puntilla* in abattoirs to help train bullfighters.

'LIFE IN PAIN'

Recently, a century's worth of accurate accounts of bullfights in the bullring at Mont-de-Marsan provided usable numerical data for over 800 bulls,[39] which made it possible to sound the depths figuratively: if all the wounds were added together, they would form a single hole about 1.45 metres deep, in other words the animal's height measured at the withers. The anatomical strategy underpinning the bullfight consisted in preserving the powerful appearance of the bull to avoid 'intolerable pity'. Massive blood loss would have been too reminiscent of butchering animals for food, and the blood had to be 'decorative'. The length of the spectacle was limited by the intelligence of the bull, which could work out what was happening in about a quarter of an hour. It realized that it had to aim for the man, not the lure. There were two prerequisites for making this butchery into a spectacle: the animal had to be kept alive long enough for the spectators to watch; but it had to be 'in pain', so that it was forced to defend itself. The art of 'maintaining life in pain' is a key technical requirement of the *corrida*.

THE ECONOMICS

This is the spectacle that established itself as a highly successful form of entertainment in Spanish cities and towns. The *Diario de Madrid* newspaper rallied to the cause of the *corrida* around 1780. Its practical commentaries listed the individual blows inflicted on the bull, for example: '10 *picas* and 15 *banderillas* . . . killed on the first *estocada* by Joseph Romero'.[40] Around this period, the bull would receive at least ten shallow lance wounds, and as many as seven *banderillas de fuego*, which were *banderillas* with firecrackers attached (20 June 1793). The profits shown for

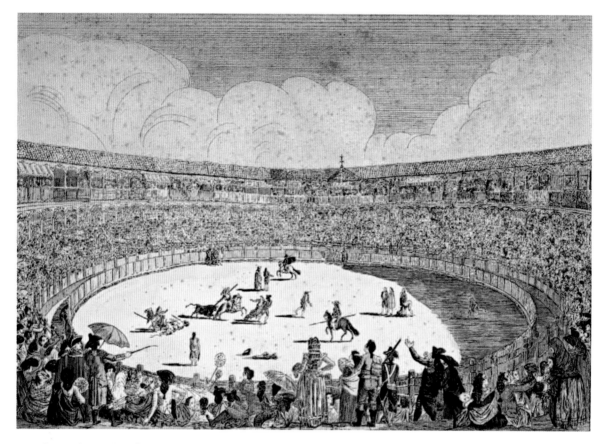

Antonio Carnicero, *View of the Bullring in Madrid*, 1791, polychrome etching.

bullfights in Madrid from 1790 to 1795, for six seasons of sixteen *corridas*, reached the incredible total of 9,251,037 *reales* (in other words, about 1,541,839 *reales* per year). Out of this sum, 69,6459,23 *reales* seem to have been paid to the Royal Hospital, and 139,729,13 *reales* was used to rebuild the monastery of the Padres Agonizantes (1789–1790).[41] However, between 1790 and 1795, takings dropped to an annual figure of 229,794 *reales*. An anonymous traveller estimated that around a third to a half of all money received was pocketed as a result of the usual corruption. Around 1790, evening *corridas* were almost twice as expensive as *corridas* held in the morning (expensive seats: 120/220 *reales*; cheaper seats: 2/4 *reales*). The seats in the sun cost 2 *reales* compared to 3 *reales* in the shade (expensive seats 70/120 *reales*). In 1786, prices ranged between 5 and 344 *reales*. The aristocratic spectacles mounted on the Plaza Mayor on 15 September 1789, were exorbitant, costing from 1,500 to 14 *reales* in the morning and from 1,000 to 28 *reales* in the afternoon. Admission charges and bull meat (10.28 per cent) accounted for 88.74 per cent of the takings. Horse skin only accounted for 0.85 per cent of the revenue. The itemized expenses for all the *corridas* of 1785 printed in the *Diario de Madrid* rose to 683,324 *reales*.[42] The *toreros* and their *cuadrilla* accounted for 20.97 per cent of expenses, the bull 2.38 per cent, the *banderillero* 0.89 per cent, which surprisingly represented the value of the horse.

Seven or eight matadors dominated the bullring: Pepe-Hillo headed the bill with around 128 bullfights, Costillares and three of the Romero family participated in over 100 spectacles, and Pedro notched up 156 bullfights, with the Andalusians leading the field. Nearly 250 cattle ranches were listed over a period of fifteen years. Advertisements for *corridas* provided extremely detailed information about the bullfighters and the bulls. They cleverly published the spectacular profits, and the tremendous fortunes made by men of

modest social origins fuelled a tremendously effective advertising campaign. The legendary rise of José Delgado, who became known as Pepe-Hillo, peaked when his wages hit 28,000 *reales* for 14 *corridas* and 30,800 *reales* in 1800. Bullfighting increased the vast disparity in wages. A barber in Madrid provided for his family on 4,500 *reales* a year. The 2,800 *reales* earned for a single *corrida* by Pepe-Hillo represented two to three times the annual pay of a cowherd from Extremadura (1,100 *reales* per year). In 1801, Pepe-Hillo's huge debts may account for the extravagant carelessness that led to his death in the bullring. His estate yielded the Spanish state 185,339 *reales* in taxes and both his accident

Zoe Leonard, *Bullfight no. 2*, 1986/1990, gelatin silver print.

and his posthumous engraved portraits were announced in the *Diario*, just as the engravings by the Spanish painter Antonio Carnicero had been. Matadors fought until they were over 50 years of age. Subsequently, matadors' fees rose initially before 1850, then again more considerably around 1880 and soared in 1890.[43] In Madrid, the season's contracts reached 10,000 *reales* around 1856 and rose to over 20,000 *reales* around 1888.

The archives of licences granted for the organization of *corridas* show that the first institutions which filed these requests were brotherhoods or religious orders who, with the state, maintained the hospitals. Then the requests became more diverse, for example, to repair war damage. Around 1830, disamortization speeded up secularization; *corridas* were held to finance roads or markets and, after 1870, the reasons became even more varied, and the spectacle went from strength to strength due to natural disasters and epidemics, cholera (1885), shipwrecks (1895), and floods (1899).

Adrian Shubert's *Death and Money in the Afternoon*, its title a parody of Hemingway's *Death in the Afternoon*, is an economic study that completely destroys the myth that a passion for bullfighting could raise mountains; in fact, the only mountains that were raised were mountains of cash. The numerous economic players involved in the *corrida* were actually depending on the durability of a spectacle so profitable that it took only a few years to recoup the cost of building a bullring.

From this point of view, bullfighting was a part of capitalism's future, although, by its very nature, the spectacle was rooted firmly in the past. It was a hymn to violence with its bladed weapons, its associations with war, its stardom, its machismo and its blatant, trivialized and institutionalized cruelty. This is probably why Enlightenment thinkers, and even one Pope, rejected a spectacle that could be encapsulated by Michel Foucault's definition of torture: 'maintaining life in pain'.

two

Capital Punishment

Public executions involving torture were a commonplace sight in many towns in southern Europe with civil or religious courts. Crowds flocked to see these 'festivals', which were so popular that they were parodied in carnivals, plays and operas. Whether knowingly or not, bullfights imitated these executions, adopting their language and behaviour, from the preparation of the prisoners to their eventual execution. The deaths of both people and animals were deferred for as long as possible, and they elicited much the same reaction from the crowd.

THE INQUISITION AT WORK

In Spain, one scholar declared that the *autos-da-fe* celebrated by the Inquisition were rivalling the celebrations of sovereignty 'where the blood of bulls is spilled'.[1] In Seville, an eye-witness account of the Inquisitorial execution of a 'witch', a young blind woman named Maria de los Dolorès Lopez, in Triana, a suburb of Seville, on 24 August 1781, was sent to Jovellanos, a friend of Francisco Goya, who was just as horrified by the Inquisition as he was by the *corrida*. This account of her execution was published in the nineteenth century by Antoine de Latour.

In Latin America, the Inquisition had three seats – in Peru, Mexico and Colombia – at which *autos-da-fé* were held.[2] In the eighteenth century

one priest, Francisco de Isla,[3] noticed a subtle analogy between the language of the Inquisition and that of the bullfight: 'the bullock was relaxed into the arm of the crowd'. As Adrian Shubert has pointed out, the selection of words was very deliberate: when the Inquisition condemned someone to death it 'relaxed' the victim into the 'secular arm', so that the state, not the Church, was responsible for the execution.

The clearest link established by contemporaries between public executions and bullfights was superbly expressed by Jean-François Bourgoing. This sensitive, erudite individual, an embassy secretary, had been in Spain since 1777. He had learned the language and took a strong interest in Spanish customs. 'Two institutions' in particular, he wrote, had more than one point in common:

> Both . . . are barbarous; one with respect to morals, and the other with respect to opinions. Neither ought to have any apologists but executioners, and yet Christian charity is the motive and excuse for both. By one, faith is armed with rigour against incredulity; and from the produce of the other, charity is enabled to assist the unfortunate. One operates as a check to the improvement of agriculture, and the other is the greatest obstacle to

sound philosophy. Is it necessary to say that one is the Inquisition and the other the bull-fights?[4]

At this time, animal protection was an anti-establishment approach that was only beginning to be espoused by thinkers like Rousseau or Bentham, forerunners of a public awareness of animal suffering. Fleuriot de Langle was one of the first Frenchmen to oppose both the *corrida* and the death penalty. Numerous travellers to Spain spiced up their written accounts by adding an account of a public execution to that of bullfighting. Long before the abolition of public executions in 1939, the physician Georges Clémenceau was stressing the links between public executions and bullfighting.[5] The novel by the Spaniard Blasco Ibanez analysed the connection between the two: the matador's

physician says 'the *autos da fé*, and executions by the burning of men, were spectacles so satisfying as to eliminate interest in mere games played with simple wild animals. The Inquisition gave birth to our grand national fiesta.'[6]

CUSTOMS IN COMMON

Hemingway himself was struck by the similarities between the structure of the *corrida* and a public execution: 'The first act [of the *corrida*] is the trial, the second act is the sentencing and the third the execution'.[7] In the Tercio de Varas, the first act with lances, the bull becomes guilty by killing the horse, then the Tercio de Banderillas represents its judgement bristling with accusations, and the sentencing is immediately followed by its execution in the third Tercio. Even better, Hemingway established a subtle link between a public execution – a crucifixion, no less –

The Execution of Robert-François Damiens, Place de Grève, Paris, 1757, print.

Francisco Goya, *Death of a Picador*, 1793–4, oil on canvas.

and a bullfight. He drew his inspiration from a crucifixion in an (unidentified) Goya painting that he deemed ferociously anticlerical: Hemingway suspected Goya of enjoying the torture he was painting with such exaggerated realism. This painting, which exuded a cynical romanticism, could serve as a poster to advertise crucifixions in the same way as bullfights were advertised: 'A crucifixion of six carefully selected Christs . . . in the Monumental Golgotha of Madrid, government permission having been obtained. The following well-known, accredited and notable crucifiers will officiate, each accompanied by his cuadrilla of nailers, hammerers, cross-raisers and spade-men, etc.[8]

In the eighteenth century, public executions were frequently parodied in carnivals, where puppets, sentenced to death, were ceremoniously burned at the stake. Animals also suffered the same fate, sometimes assuaging a desire for revenge: the cat belonging to a printer that was seized by his discontented workers was hung after its trial, confession and sentencing. Moratín wrote in his diary that executions reconstructed in minute detail on the theatre stage were a huge success. In the nineteenth century operas included executions performed in the wings and sometimes even on stage, and these are still played to this day. In the *Dialogue des Carmélites* by Bernanos, the revolutionary scaffold is not far off, and some productions (Paris, 1952) allow the audience to hear the dull thud of falling heads.

Citizens in Spain's cities were accustomed to watching executions. No one seemed to miss these events, to judge from the size of the crowds that flocked to witness them; people sometimes even turned up the evening before to make sure of securing a good view. Well-documented historical studies reveal that the frequency of executions

Louis-Dominique Bourguignon ('Cartouche'), *Crowd at an Execution, Place de Grève, Paris, 1721*, print. *c.* 1578, engraving.

and their high attendance was common throughout Europe. In Toulouse, for example, one could see around seven executions per year in the seventeenth century, while in Amsterdam the number ranged from 15 to 30.[9] In London, advertisements of executions drew estimated crowds of 100,000 spectators.[10] If the condemned prisoner was pardoned at the last minute, the disappointed crowd often rioted. In 1781 in Seville's Triana suburb, from dawn 'the boats swayed under the number of people': because the bridges were packed, the Inquisitors had to travel by boat to the blind María de los Dolorès

José Solana, *The Cartel of Crime*, c. 1932–3, etching. Passers-by reading the notice of a public torture and execution, describing the wrongdoings of the prisoners, set to ballads performed by blind singers.

López's place of execution. A public execution had to be slow if it was to constitute a spectacle: 'Our guillotine isn't bad, but it's quick as a flash', declared Clémenceau and, in fact, the carts carrying the prisoners condemned during the French Revolution took the longest route, solely to meet the needs of a spectacle that was supposed to set an example.[11] When on one occasion an inexperienced executioner blundered and instantly killed a man tied to the wheel, he was noisily booed by the crowd.[12] The same response occurred when a picador killed the bull. Without a slow death there was no spectacle, without a standing, snorting bull there was no bullfight. Executions had to be slow. When a hand was severed from a condemned man to overcome resistance, a surgeon followed the executioner so that he could apply a tourniquet to stop the victim suddenly bleeding to death. The condemned, whether it was a man, or a bull spiked with *banderillas*, were forced into a prolonged agony.

In all likelihood, a condemned prisoner and a bull were prepared for their public appearance in similar ways, because these methods shared a common goal: to weaken the victim. First, the condemned were kept isolated for some time:

The dart of a *banderilla*.

according to the French scholar Antoine de Latour, writing in 1863, it was common practice in Spain to keep a prisoner sequestered for 'three days of supreme hardship'; an animal, similarly, was shut in a dark *toril* or bullpen. In preparation for the execution, the condemned man's hair was shaved or cut; and, either in ironic imitation or by coincidence, the procedure that involved shortening the bull's horns was called *afeitar*, a Spanish word meaning 'to shave'. Finally, there was the prisoner's ultimate costume. Certain costumes symbolized the crime, for example, the yellow outfit worn by those who had committed murder by treason. Others made the condemned man the member of an honourable social group, whose uniform he would wear when dead. The condemned blind woman in Triana was attired in the black habit of the Sisters of Charity. The bull had a lance with a 7-cm blade, the *divisa*, thrust below its shoulder blade, fluttering with ribbons in the colours of its donor, its breeder.

With this new identity, the bull became a member of a human group to which it was supposed to owe its life and, by extension, its death. The costuming of the condemned man or animal showed that the victims had been appropriated by the social group that had sentenced him or it to death.

It should be added that the bull, like the convict or galley slave, had also been branded in accordance with a law situating it within a human place and time. Like an insubordinate serf whose ears were cropped in disgrace, a disfigurement that functioned like a criminal record, the animal had an *escoussure* or cut on its ear to identify its owner. The condemned bull was then ready, and the gate of the bullpen could be opened.

AT THE KILL

In executions, to clear society of any blame, the condemned man had to accept his fate. The bull

Sergui Chepnik, *Tauromachia*, 1992, mixed media on canvas.

also had to submit. The bullfighting *aficionado* believes that the bull, when it appears submissive, becomes a 'complicit animal, consenting to the sweet intoxication, the true enchantment wrought by a love of bodies caressed, concealed, rediscov-ered'.[13] In this phase of the bullfight, the dying, breathless bull, bristling with weapons, is covered with blood and uses its last reserves of strength for a pathetic, pitiful defence. However, if the bull resorted to its natural form of defence,

Tony Quimbel, *Injury and Adoration*, 2006, oil on canvas.

by fleeing as opposed to attacking, he betrayed man's cause: 'This bull that he treated like a friend, like a collaborator in his work, rebelled and acted like a traitor'.[14] He was called *manso* (cowardly) and 'punished', which is the accepted word in both bullfighting and the penal system. As in a public execution, the bull was tortured further, formerly by *banderillas de fuego*, or attacked by the abattoir watchdogs.

Any type of execution gives rise to an impressive silence. However, if the executioner botched the execution, the crowd would turn against him; in the seventeenth century, one executioner was lynched by the crowd and died before the condemned prisoner. Hapless matadors who botch the bull's execution are booed. Sofsky brilliantly analyzes the way crowds can turn, formerly at executions and now at bullfights:

> By ostracizing the executioner on account of violence – a violence that they themselves initiated – they acquit themselves. By displacing the rage and fear, the spectator is no longer divided. He can now happily enjoy the terror . . . All eyes are turned on death. The nearer it comes, the greater the tension waiting for release . . . when it comes . . . a cry rises from the crowd. If the executioner

has done well, the ovations turn into a celebration of the people . . . 'gallows beer' is served . . . people buy souvenirs.[15]

The 'voice of the crowd' rises from the bullrings and can be heard from a great distance: 'It is a cry of terror, fear and freedom'.[16]

After beheadings, the head of the condemned prisoner used to be brandished aloft; in the bullrings, the matador, who is rewarded at the crowd's request, brandishes the bull's ears, tail and on occasion its leg. If the bull has been aggressive, its bloody corpse is paraded on a lap of honour. The bull sported colours embedded in its flesh which were not its own; it was subjected to all the different phases of a public execution and described using legal jargon. The final turnaround was striking: the participants were partaking of a pleasure that cost nothing and was even sanctioned by indulgences from the Church – while others, the spectators, comfortably seated on their tiered seats, had paid to watch and were thereby subsidizing a form of torture that they would suddenly boo, then cheer on again, yelling at the sight of the bloody trophies. These striking similarities have been highlighted by recent historical studies on public executions. It is not clear, though, whether this similarity between bullfights and public executions is the result of a simple causal relationship, shared theatrical requirements or a well-planned scenario.

OPPOSITION

If drawing parallels between public executions and bullfights may seem surprising today, it was once obvious, which is why opponents of executions were also opposed to bullfighting. The majority of Spanish intellectuals and the kings of the Bourbon dynasty, who began ruling

Alexander von Wagner's illustration of passers-by reading a poster advertising a bullfight, from Théodore Simons's *L'Espagne* (1884).

in Spain with Philip v, were horrified by the bloody bullfights. Faced with the practical impossibility of an immediate ban, due to their great popularity, Philip v decreed a partial ban in

Bilbao bullfighting calendar for September 1944.

Oswaldo Guayasamín, *Bullfight*, 1947, oil on canvas.

Oscar Dominguez, *Bullfight*, 1947, lithograph.

1725 in a bid to restrict them gradually. Ferdinand vi followed suit in 1754, although he made a contribution to the reconstruction of the extremely profitable bullring in Madrid. Under Charles iii, two sessions of the Council of Castile were chaired by the Count of Aranda (1767–8, 1774).[17] The discussions resulted in the law of 9 November 1786, which banned bullfighting in the kingdom. However, this was only partially enforced, due to deep-seated cruelty, the subterfuge of charitable work and, around 1790, a developing regionalization. Several members of the Council had suggested that bullfighting be abolished gradually over a period of four years. Manuel Ventura Figueroa declared that only 'inhumanity could appreciate the spectacle'.

The most durable argument, which was still being employed in the early twentieth century, was the economic damage done by bullfighting. The artisans were impoverished and the ranches made losses because of the long distances travelled to the bullring, alcoholism, and the fact that Mondays were sometimes taken as public holidays at the request of the Church. In farming, a bull cost more than 50 draught cattle and grazed to the detriment of useful cattle. According to the figures cited, some 1,800 bulls and 500 horses were killed per year in 185 villages, not including local fiestas. However, one of the few apologists of bullfighting countered these figures with the 2,554,920 *reales* profit made on admission fees at the Maestranza in Seville. Jovellanos ran through his political arguments. Europe regarded the whole of Spain as barbaric, although *corridas* were only held irregularly outside Cadiz and Madrid. The sight of people leaving the bullrings was enough to demonstrate the ill effects of excessive alcohol consumption, overeating, excitement and violence. The decree (Cedula) of 10 February 1805 introduced widespread cultural reform, including a total ban on bullfighting. Godoy, Charles IV's minister, focused on the courage of a king daring to brave unpopularity 'by rooting out a vice in humanity that borders on the irrational'. He asked 'Isn't there a certain cruelty about such bloody spectacles that familiarizes people with bloodshed and the sufferings of their fellow man? Will the atrocities committed by the civil war in the unhappy days we lived through ever stop demonstrating that the Spanish character needs to be softened in place of these blood-thirsty festivals and diversions?'[18] The Inquisition was abolished after Napoleon placed José Bonaparte on the Spanish throne, but bullfighting was soon reinstated.

The eighteenth-century Church made a great deal of profit from bullfighting through its ranches, its lands, its bullrings on occasion, its convents and its bullfights, which were sometimes even granted indulgences when it came to building the Franciscan convent in Madrid. The ban issued by Pius V back in 1567, the so-called *De Salute Gregis* bull, was completely ignored, even though, according to canon law, Papal Bulls last in perpetuity.

Pius V's ban is a text whose bravery and profundity ought not to be obscured by the vocabulary of the period, or by the fact that its severity subsequently had to be toned down. With his sights set on Portugal, the despot Philip II defended his noble cavalry, key participants in the bullfights, and then his troops laid siege

to the Papal states. The following Papal Texts (Gregory XIII, 1575; Sixtus V, Clement VIII, 1596) were less severe, so that in the end virtually all clergymen were authorized to attend bullfights. As a result, after 40 years and three popes the majority of clergymen were allowed to attend a morally unacceptable festival, whose perverse nature had been revealed, named and stigmatized by a canonized pope.

Jean Baudrillard voices an anthropological fact which is more suitable for our secular society than the albeit perceptive imprecations of a sixteenth-century pope: 'It is the application of a *human* ceremonial to a beast that . . . gives the scene its extraordinary atrocity . . . every attempt to dress an animal, every disguise and attempt to tame an animal to the human comedy is sinister and unhealthy. By dying, it would become frankly unbearable.'[19]

three

Plazas and Bullrings

PLAZAS

In Spain, rulers held lavish festivals on public squares, such as the Plaza Mayor in Madrid. Both in Spain and Latin America, the main square in any city, the *plaza*, was the site for all gatherings, whether celebratory or sad, political or mercantile. For bull festivals, the square was temporarily closed and, in the fairly wealthy towns, carpenters were paid to make the wooden terraces. The first plans for Madrid's Plaza Mayor by Juan de Herrera, around 1581, completed under Philip II, around 1590, included a bakery to the north and the town's butchers' shops to the south, lined with shady arcades. When the Royal Court took up residence in Madrid in the seventeenth century, the Plaza acquired a celebratory function. Staircases were added leading to the second floor of the bakery, whose occupants were temporarily evicted; the balconies were requisitioned and the king purchased the one belonging to the *panadería*. A century later, the monumental square was brightly painted in reds, blacks and golds, which were offset by the green covering on the ground. Madrid's Plaza Mayor became the *representatio majestatis* of the King of Spain and America. The architecture was hidden by the temporary fixtures for the festivals, but hangings bore the royal colours at the celebrations of sovereignty, where the bulls were killed. It took days of work to seat the 544 guests in protocol order on the wooden terraces at the festival of 1746.[1]

BULLRINGS

The layout of the temporary wooden terraces propped up against the stone facades was imitated for the early bullrings, which were built with boxes at the top, followed by *tendidos* (tiered seats) and barriers at the bottom. Around 1710 in Madrid an impregnable wall barred access to people wanting to sneak in without paying, while enclosing men and animals in an arena, for money. The bullring was born.

The bullrings that followed were stone reproductions of the temporary layout of the Plaza Mayor, although circular in plan.[2] In the bullring, boxes, balconies or *palcos* corresponded to the stone balconies in the Plaza Mayor; terraced seats, the bullring's *graderia*, corresponded to the covered terraces made of wood; and the bullring's *tendidos* corresponded to the open wooden terraces. Finally, both monuments featured the wooden fences, the *barreras*, at the bottom. Most bullrings adopted this prototype.

A bullring often started life with an impregnable circular surrounding wall, equipped on the inside with rudimentary wooden terraces. Every period left its stylistic stamp, which found expression in the supports, from the fine neoclassical

Alfred Dehodencq, *Bullfight in Spain*, 1850–51, oil on canvas.

José Solana, *Plaza de las Ventas*, 1907, oil on canvas.

The bullring in Ronda, c. 1950.

columns in Ronda to the cast-iron supports widely used that appeared before 1900. Temporary bullrings, made entirely of wood, were simpler in appearance; in Cuenca (Peru), for the bullfighting festival of 1739,[3] the boxes were composed of six-metre-high vertical girders, decorated with hangings, overlooking a quadrangular bullring, like the first Maestranza of Seville (1761). There was a huge wooden bullring in Bilbao (Spain), seating 9,000, which was vulnerable to fire because so many of those that attended it smoked tobacco and were often intoxicated. The Falcon bullring in Caracas burned down in 1868. Mexico had numerous wooden bullrings in 1955: these structures were more popular there as they were better able to withstand earthquakes. Traditional adobes (bricks of dried earth) were used for the small bullrings. The use of brick made it possible to create Mudéjar pastiches (the Islamic-inspired style of architecture of Spain's long Middle Ages), in keeping with the ambiance in the city of Granada, although less expected in Colombia's capital, Bogotá.[4] Barcelona's red-brick bullring reflected the Moorish style reinterpreted by Gaudí. Mexico City's Plaza Monumental bullring required a team of architects and engineers.

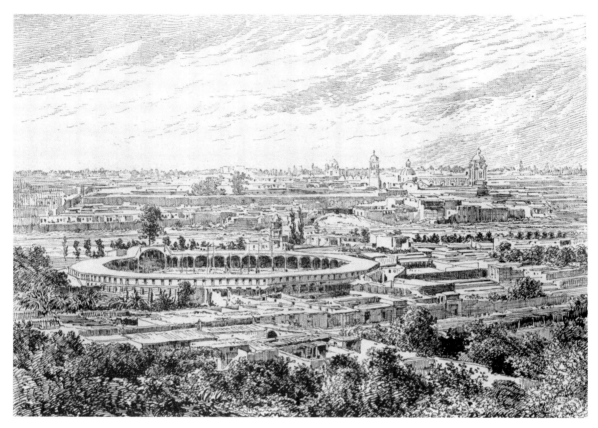

Attrib. D. Lancelot, 'General view of Lima with the Plaza de Hacho in the foreground', illustration for Charles Wiener, *Pérou et Bolivie, récit de voyage . . .* (1880).

The temporary conversion of public squares was universally expensive and problematic and did not adequately satisfy the technical requirements of the new style of bullfighting. In Mexico City a profitability study was carried out before the construction of the permanent bullring planned for San Pablo (*c.* 1788). The revenue generated by 40 annual bullfights financed the Chapultepec Palace, built by the viceroys (*virreys*) of New Spain. The bullrings, which were smaller than those in Europe, were better suited for fighting the weaker Mexican bulls. The profitability of octagonal bullrings was compared to oval ones: corners were avoided because they could provide the bulls with a place of refuge. Bullfighting spectacles began to charge an admission fee earlier in South America than in Europe because, from the twelfth century onwards, the *cabildos* or councils had to be self-supporting, without any assistance from an inaccessible monarch.[5] A bullring in Canadas in Mexico is thought to date from 1680, but it is not known what spectacles were held there. Seville (1707) and Caracas (1708), Huelva Calpofrio (Extremadura, Spain) and the Alcalá bullring in Madrid were built when mounted bullfighting or *rejón* was on the decline. One characteristic feature of the bullring was an effective method of locking the gates.

On one occasion, the racecourse in Caracas, which did not have effective gates, was overrun by 2,000 people who sneaked in without paying and who were battled by 1,750 paying ticket-holders!

The largest and earliest bullring in Latin America, in Lima, Peru, began life with a charitable fund established by the Creole aristocrat Inez Unoz de la River, who founded the convent of La Concepción on the slopes of Mt Cristobal, on the right bank of the Rimac. On the high site of Acho (peak), a temporary wooden bullring (1537) was authorized for eight spectacles and an *encierro*. One of the owner's descendants in the Caneta Valley rebuilt it in brick in 1765, then enclosed it in 1793, to make sure that only paying customers gained entry. He shared the profits generated by bullfighting and cockfighting spectacles with a hospice for the poor. After a detailed enquiry into its real cost, a royal decree arrived from Aranjuez in 1803. The owner, Agustin Landaburu, who had been compromised in Spain, died in exile in London in 1817. A decree of 20 September 1817 gave the bullring to the government of Lima.[6] The third largest bullring in the world, the bullring at Acho, appears originally to have measured just over 100 metres in diameter (around 320 metres in circumference), and the height to the galleries was just over 5 metres. Its first season of spectacles (1809–10) brought in a quarter of the cost of construction back in 1765, which demonstrates the precocious profitability of Latin American bullfighting.

There were various bullring developers in Spain. In the turmoil of the Spanish disamortization, members of religious orders built bullrings under the pretext of carrying out charity work, like the present-day Casa de Misericordia in Pamplona. Various municipal authorities (Senà, Fuentes de Léon, Extremadura) used land that

William Walcot, *Bullfight, Seville*, c. 1922, etching.

had once been a corral. One renowned breeder, the Duke of Veragua, requested a licence in 1894. There were bullrings in Seville and in Caracas, Venezuela, before 1720; in Madrid, at the Puerta de Alcalá, before 1740; in the largest Spanish cities, Seville, Madrid, Saragossa and Ronda, after 1750; and in Mexico City, Lima and Guatemala, where bullfighting was soon stopped. Subsequently construction projects increased, and a Spanish matador joined forces with a banker in Mexico City in 1913. Around 1950, several building companies (El Toreo de Puebla SA) saturated the Mexican market.[7] In 1993 the famous Colombian matador, César Rincón, opened his bullring near Bogotá at Duitama, Colombia.

Bullrings became an established architectural feature during the rapid urbanization of the eighteenth century; towns became important places of power. In Venezuela, the rural aristocracy took up residence in the city. A handful of the 658 families in Venezuela (1.5 per cent of the population) owned all the arable and grazing lands, and lived in Caracas.[8] Tightly enclosed within their surrounding blind walls (like Talavera de la

The bullring in Malaga, *c.* 1870.

Plaza de Toros, Madrid.

Reina), the bullrings tended to communicate with the town via a monumental entrance, adorned with figures of bulls that evoked a vanished rural life (although there were also discreet service entrances). Unlike the zoos, which were still open, the bullrings, which usually stood empty, were filled on occasion with frenzied, bawling crowds. The racecourses were situated further out, cutting into the countryside. In Buenos Aires, which became the capital of the province of Rio de la Plata in 1779, the bullring built in the Montserrat district in 1791 provoked complaints: the dead bulls stank and robbery became rife. The bullring's Moorish facade was destroyed by the British invasion in 1801 and bullfights were banned. On rare occasions, urban development was boosted by the bullring. In Mexico City, a tobacco factory was built adjacent to the bullring and, in Seville, the Maestranza developed the insalubrious banks of the Tagus for its arena, regenerating an entire district.

In Spanish, the bullring is still called *plaza*, the meaning of the word having shifted onto the actual building constructed to accommodate the bullfights. The French still use the word *arène*, from the Latin for sand. The bullring has several things in common with the ancient Roman arena: its circular shape, the tiered seating for spectators, and certain types of bloodthirsty combat. However, the bullring encloses the men and animals inside with no way out, whereas the ancient arena, on the contrary, was open to everyone and allowed free movement, thereby symbolizing a unifying sovereignty. The arena was a crowd-magnet, while the bullring was a drain on finances: centripetal versus centrifugal forces. The fact that bullfighting had abandoned the public squares showed that the spectacle had broken away from public life, because it was on

the squares that they 'beheaded traitors, burned heretics at the stake . . . in short, where they set the entire liturgical machinery of the monarchy into motion'.[9] The bullring made bullfighting a permanent, firmly established part of city life. However, property developers everywhere, avid for urban spaces, kept watch on the bullrings, which, invaded by grass, reverted to pasture.[10]

THE BULL AND THE HERD

Like all domestic cattle, the bull originated in the Indies and is descended from Bos Taurus, which is thought to have produced the huge aurochs, similar to the Bison Priscus. The fighting bull is simply a *variety* obtained by breeders, who have made it more aggressive than it should naturally be, so it is not even a sub-species at the bottom of the taxonomic classification. 'Although the disappearance of several genetic varieties may be important in biological evolution, if these varieties have been created by man then they are not important', since they can be reproduced in a case of extinction.[11]

Even before Descartes described animals as machines, Spanish speakers regarded animals as unfeeling slaves.[12] 'Quadrupeds are in the service of mankind', the bullfighting treatise of 1796 proclaimed: 'The act of dominating the animals in their respective countries and regions and exploiting them is peculiar to man'.[13] In South America, slaves and animals were treated with equal cruelty by the conquistadors, who believed both to be devoid 'of common sense': 'our Spaniards believe they are entitled to treat the Indians very ill and to rank them with the animals'.[14]

In the sixteenth century, Spanish herds of cattle comprised domestic animals, milk cows and draught cattle, usually castrated and broken in

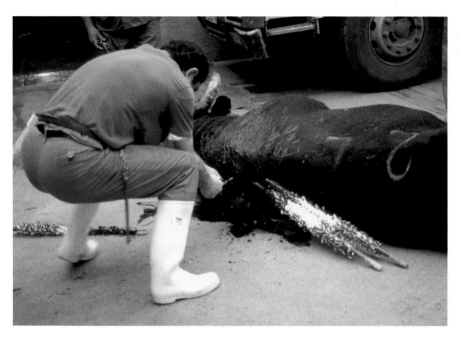

Banderillas being cut from a fighting bull in the abattoir at a Spanish bullring.

(*domado*). Bulls described as *cerril* (wild, unbroken) were stubborn animals, not easy to tame. They were kept for three years for fighting and were called *toros de muerte*. Their aggressive nature was unpredictable. Fighting a bull was tantamount to readying it for execution.[15] During this period, the cattle were branded to identify them in case of lawsuits. The blood of the herd was renewed by swapping breeder bulls. Numerous religious orders owned stud bulls, which had been obtained by means of the tithe (a tax in kind). When the Jesuits were expelled from Spain and its dominions in 1767, 'the college of Arcos had twenty-eight fighting *toros*'.[16] The clergy's financial involvement in bullfighting was therefore deeply rooted in age-old serfdom.

Before the spread of mass-produced fodder (*pienso*), the cattle were fed on hay and the leaves from trees and vines after the harvest. Some cattle were put out to pasture in uncultivated pastures (*dehesas*). These impoverished lands in western Spain, variously planted with trees and grasses, are neglected and subject to erosion, drought, excessive farming and hunting. Far from maintaining the *dehesas*, the bulls, even in small numbers, contribute to desertification: they destroy the plant coverage by grazing, they ruin the drainage by trampling the ground, and they disturb or even drive off wild animals, such as lynxes, which are becoming an endangered species, and Spanish Imperial Eagles (protected by 75 laws and regulations). As a result, breeding fighting bulls is damaging the natural plant and animal heritage of Spain. The owners of these lands could have their *dehesas* classified (25 per cent are classified) rather than using them for grazing.[17]

Spanish breeding changed in Spain with the arrival of the Bourbon king Philip v in 1700 and the War of the Spanish Succession (1702–13), which caused the Spanish nobility to flee the court in Madrid and withdraw to their rural estates.

However, the 150 ranches represented in Madrid's bullrings in the late eighteenth century only included six aristocratic breeders. During that century the price of cattle rose from 228 *reales* in 1724 to 425 in 1785. According to José Blanco White, the cost of fighting bulls doubled, from 600 to reach 1200 *reales* around 1750, and then soaring from 1,500 to 3,300 *reales* between 1814 and 1817, reaching its highest point before 1880,[18] which accounts for the considerable pressure exerted by Spanish breeders on the French market around 1889.

Two ranches specialized in fighting bulls, Vasquez (1780) and Vistahermosa (1770). They introduced innovative selection methods similar to those of Robert Bakewell in England. The pioneering Duke of Veragua avoided consanguinity and promoted crossbreeding, a practice that was rejected by the traditional aristocracy, who believed that only the male, whether horse or man, transmitted heredity. This laid the foundations for a specific breeding programme that developed in nineteenth-century Spain.

The situation was different in South America. Imported by the Spanish, the cattle were introduced onto *terra firma* after a stay in the West Indies, where they proliferated dangerously before the end of the sixteenth century.[19] 'If you allow large herds, you will destroy the Indians', warned the Spanish Virrey, Antonio de Mendoza (1550), since the cattle were destroying the Indians' food crops. The animals that escaped

Valencia, La Plaza de Toros.

from the herds reverted to their wild state and become *cimarrons* ('runaways') and, depending on their complicated crossbreeding, were called *bramino*, *cebu*, *criollo* or *ladino*.[20] Cows from Navarre, introduced by the Jesuits, had survived the expulsion of the priests in 1767 and were guarded by Spanish dogs. As prey, the *cimarrons* became legally *res nullius*: they were the property of whoever killed them in order to sell their horns and hide, products that were exported to Cadiz in their hundreds of thousands every year.[21]

The myth of the savage wild bull that had disappeared from Spain centuries ago grew in the American imagination. In Mexico, Jacques Soustelle recorded in 1933 the *Danza del torito*, which relates and mimics in heroic style the adventures of the wild *Torito*, captured by lariat, then killed and dismembered.[22] The so-called wild nature of Spanish bulls served to increase the theatrical effect of their dangerousness and, in France, was used to avoid enforcing the Loi Grammont, which was restricted to domestic animals.

The South American uplands were better suited to cattle, for example the plateaux of the Mexican Anahuac. The *altiplanos* in Ecuador produced smaller bulls than the lowlands with their polluted waters overrun with parasites. In Colombia, the best altitude was around 2,500 metres. In Bolivia, in 1843, Castelnau saw some 'undernourished bulls, suffering from altitude sickness, horrifying in La Paz'. The blockade of ports by Louis Philip in 1838 held up the potential importation of Spanish cattle. In 1855 fences were improved by the introduction of barbed wire, which however did not stop predators, cats or feral dogs.

Wild bulls (*cimarrons*) were not suitable for sustained combat. They protected themselves from danger by fleeing, or by a show of strength: a bull would threaten with its horns, paw the ground, bellow, and raise the crest of muscles in its neck.[23] Several travellers noticed the 'gentle and peaceable (nature) of the bulls from La Paz' in Bolivia. At one bullfighting festival at Santa Cruz de La Sierra, 'the grass looked [so] appetizing [to the bull, it] . . . began grazing.[24] In Mexico, the explorer John Lloyd Stephens[25] saw 'one poor ox' in the bullring and Charnay saw some 'bloody toros',[26] and the crowd shouted: *'fuera la vaca!'* Saussure believed that 'if we had brought (the matadors) one of our Alpine bulls, all the matadors would have emigrated in a flash'.[27] Only cattle whose nature was constantly warped by men could acquire the continually aggressive behaviour that made them suitable for a sustained fight: 'When attacked, (wild) bulls defend themselves with a mechanism identical to that of the fighting bull . . . the radical difference is their persistence'.[28] In South America, therefore, the bulls had continually to be incited to charge. Before they entered the bullring, numerous witnesses

A Mexican bull fought in Lima, Peru, November 2006.

described them being jabbed 'to put them in a rage', often by the crowd, through the top of the cages, sometimes for hours. In Lima, 'poking' seems to have involved burning, as with a hot poker. Elsewhere, there were reports of a bull with a heavy load slung around its neck. The practice of *afeitado* (shortening the horns) was regarded as a 'sensible precaution' in Bogotá,[29] Mexico,[30] Venezuela[31] and Peru,[32] and Loewenstern wrote 'as was the custom, they had cut off the bull's horns'.[33] In the Paseo Nuevo bullring in Mexico City, the fixed price (1 per cent of costs) for hiring a bull with its horns sheathed in leather, indicated that this was standard practice.[34] Substantial use of firecrackers or fireworks kept overly peaceable bulls in a state of excitement.

Horses, imported from Spain, soon, like cattle, reverted to their wild state. When captured they were broken in by the Indians, who became skilled horsemen and herded their cattle on horseback, which was common practice throughout the Americas. This resulted in the loss of the horse as the principal identifying mark for the Latin American aristocracy and consequently the rider became symbolic of a country, rather than of a social class. It was unusual for unmounted bullfighters in Latin America to represent the vengeful lower classes, which had been the case in Spain, since they were entitled to fight on horseback, a skill at which the Indians excelled.

Ranches that specialized to some extent in breeding fighting bulls began appearing in Mexico from 1810 (San Luis Potosí); those in the Toluca valley began producing bulls in 1865 with no Spanish crossbreeding. From 1902 onwards, two of the most famous herds in Tlaxcala – La Laguna and Piedras Negras – began breeding the best fighting bulls, under the influence of the famous matador, Mazzantini.[35]

COMMERCIAL EXPLOITATION

The economic chain of the bullfighting industry implicated numerous trades. The overconsumption of meat affected South America as it did Spain. Slaughtering for food in towns was widespread, because cattle were killed in the pasturelands primarily for their tongues, a popular delicacy, and for their horns and hides, which were sent in their millions to the ports for the thriving tanning industry.[36] The German naturalist and explorer Alexander von Humboldt, like his predecessor Concolorcorvo, not only criticized the growing number of urban abattoirs, but also the cruel slaughter that was practised secretly in the prairies: the bull was immobilized, either with a lasso or by hamstringing the animal with a *media luna* (crescent-shaped knife); it was flayed alive, its tongue was eaten, wild dogs and

Advertisement for 'meat tenderizer' in the *Saturday Evening Post* (1954).

Outside and within the arena at Nîmes.

vultures devoured the rest and its bones were left strewn over the pasturelands. Meat began to be industrialized in Mexico from the eighteenth century; industrial refrigeration made its appearance in the 1870s, at a time when bullfighting was spreading in Latin America. As a result, people were in the habit of regarding cattle merely as a consumer product to be killed as they liked.

The link between bullfighting and tobacco was less direct and rarely mentioned, despite the fact that two tobacco factories were constructed adjacent to two major bullrings (Seville and Mexico City). On the wooden terraces, heavy smoking, though a fire hazard, was not controlled. In literature, and later in poster advertising, the famous cigarette girl Carmen became the emblematic French gypsy found on the blue packet of the time-honoured cigarette brand Gitanes. Advertisements for tobacco, whether beautiful (Colin) or amusing (Yoldjoglou), depicted or alluded to bullfighting; the French cigarette-maker Seita subsidized bullfighting for many years.

Finally, the bullring was a productive point of sale for a host of small retailers, as depicted by the artist Léonce Angrand in Lima. Very strong alcohol did the rounds on the terraces. Wine and alcohol were often produced by cattle ranches. Around 1990, crowds of spectators at the entrance gates to the bullring in Madrid could be seen openly carrying a great deal of alcohol for consumption within the arena.

Engravings on the subject of bullfighting were a lucrative by-product of the sport, particularly in Spain and England. In the eighteenth century, this effective dissemination tool went hand in hand with a general interest in popular life. In Spain, the royal tapestry-making factories

Le Toreador de Carmen, c. 1890, cover for printed music.

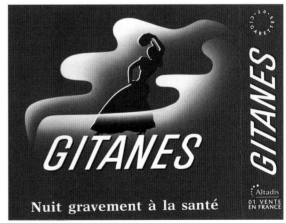

Gitanes packet.

Frontispiece to Antonio Carnicero, *Collection of the Main Actions in a Bullfight*, 1790, hand-coloured etching.

commissioned scenes of popular life from painters like Antonio Carnicero (1736–1804) and Goya, who was asked to depict a *novillada*. In France, the small trades of the populace were illustrated and published in the *Cris de Paris*. In Spain, the book on horsemanship *Exercicios de la Gineta*, illustrated with engravings by Maria Eugenia de Beer, showed a man confronting an animal with an intricately described weapon in a situation resembling a bullfight.

In 1787 Antonio Carnicero engraved and sold several plates depicting bullfighting, featured in the *Diario de Madrid*.[37] The bullring was well-suited to the perspective views in fashion at the time. By the end of the century, works on Spain featured engravings of bullfighting: Edgar Orme's

illustrated book was published in London in 1813, three years earlier than Goya's *Tauromaquia*. A few years earlier, in 1790, a set of hand-coloured pen-and-ink drawings by Antonio Carnicero, depicting scenes from a bullfight, were etched and published.[38] In 1804, 30 of these etchings were used to illustrate the second Madrid edition of *El arte de torerar* by Pepe-Hillo. The consummate technical nature of these illustrations helped to consolidate the spectacle. Carnicero's illustrations became the benchmark, from the worst *kitsch* to the *Picador* by Delacroix, who found his inspiration for his hand-coloured drawing in Carnicero's work.[39]

Eugène Delacroix, *The Picador*, 1832, watercolour.

four

What Travellers Saw

The end of the Napoleonic War in 1815 and the beginning of civil liberties in the 1820s in Latin America marked an escalation in the number of voyages and expeditions made there, the travelogues published about them, and the commercial and political links established. Nineteenth-century visitors wrote accounts of various bullfighting spectacles, although they tended to prefer Indian festivals to bullfights in large arenas. The *Relaciones Geográficas*, an important series of regional guides produced by various administrations, provide detailed information about Spanish rule in South America and certain religious festivals. A fairly early account of a Peruvian bullfighting festival figured in a police enquiry into the murder of Dr Seniergues, a member of the expedition that had been sent to measure the Earth at the equator. He was killed during a bullfighting festival held in August 1739, in Cuenca (Peru), by armed spectators attending a 'Mudéjar style' show of horsemanship with bulls.[1] Celebrations of sovereignty were held in South America as in Spain, along with so many other festivals that, in Colombia, half the year was spent in celebration![2] With the king so far away, this was how the South American viceroys asserted their authority in order to play down and avert danger, and make the populace forget their fears. The frequent festive military parades were intended to provide reassurance and curb any insurrectional impulses.[3]

Alexander von Humboldt won renown for his exploration of the perilous uncharted lands of the interior. His final, pioneering investigative report on Mexico, published in London in the early nineteenth century, showed a lively interest in everything except the entertainments, whether they involved bullfighting or not. He saw the bullring in Lima, but it is not known whether he attended any bullfights to celebrate his first ascent of volcanic Chimborazo (August 1802). In Cartagena he found the Indian festivities to be a 'barbarous spectacle . . . incapable of softening manners'.[4]

Travel books, published in greater numbers in the nineteenth century, preferred Indian festivals and cockfighting to bullfighting. Bulls were mentioned in around 50 books. Each continent had its own preferred style of fighting in wartime: the Europeans ran their enemies through; the South Americans used rope to capture them alive and then exploited them. Everywhere, bladed weapons held their own against firearms. An American battle of June 1824 resembled a romantic Spanish bullfight at which one could hear 'the clash of swords and lances, the horses galloping, the oaths of the defeated, the moans of the wounded'.[5]

Jean-Baptiste Tardieu, *A Square Prepared for a Bullfight, Cuenca, Peru*, 1778, print.

The Indian weapon for fighting and hunting was the *lazo* or lasso, and its effectiveness was improved by the use of Spanish horses, which increased the thrower's speed, and by the use of bull hide cut into a coil, which made for sturdier, longer lassos (18 to 20 metres, according to John Lloyd Stephens in 1841). The *rosario*, with two balls (*bolas*) and the *ramales*, with three balls at one end, made of stone or pierced horns, could knock out or choke victims. The lasso, whether plain or decorated, was thrown skilfully as the horse circled at speed. The thrower aimed for the bull's horns (*cabeza*), or its front legs (*mangana*) or back legs. The horses, accustomed to the impact, seemed to become one with their rider to withstand the shock. A special heavy harness was equipped with a ring attaching it to the saddle.[6] The bull, still standing, was tied to the horse's tail. It could take ten men to catch a bull, according to Paul Walle, in Bolivia (1911). The majestic setting of the Hacienda de Naranjo impressed traveller John Lloyd Stephens near Guatemala in the early 1840s: 'Two horsemen followed and drove him out . . . in a few moments the *lazo* whizzed over his head, and, while horse and rider stood like marble, the ox again came with a plunge to the ground'.[7] This activity became a form of entertainment, sometimes as part of a bullfight, but especially as part of the *charreria* (a show of horsemanship). In the *coleado*, the rider

Francisco Goya, *Mariano Ceballos Places Bandilleras while Mounted on a Bull*, preparatory red chalk drawing for *Tauromaquia*.

Francisco Goya, *Mariano Ceballos, Alias 'The Indian', Kills the Bull From his Horse*, preparatory red chalk drawing for *Tauromaquia*.

grabs hold of the bull's tail at top speed, overtakes it, turns back on himself and throws the animal to the ground. The bull suffers as much as in the Spanish *derribo*, where it is stabbed on the rear, beneath the tail.

The roped bull was used as a mount in the *jaripeo*, with the rider holding onto the ropes.

The bull would be covered with blood from huge spurs on the rider's sandals, as depicted by Goya. Sometimes the rider on the bull would kill another bull, then kill his mount. In Lima, the bull-rider threw flowers and played the guitar.[8] A picador straddled a bull. In Mexico City, mounted bulls moved among the crowd.[9] The *jaripeo* was an attraction (*mojigangas*) in the bullring, before the bullfight, then became a professional sport in South America. In Bogotá, the government held two *jaripeos* per year ('banning them would start a revolution'[10]). In America, *jaripeos* and bullfights were competitive.

In Spain, Mariano Ceballos (known there as 'the Indian') cut a dashing figure on his visit to Pamplona in 1775. Around 1815, Goya depicted him on five occasions in engravings, then in lithographs.[11] In 1840, the Spaniards were still searching for Indian bullfighters for their spectacles, in which they featured almost as ethnological or exotic attractions.

Cattle in Spain were tied by the horns with rope used in farming to force them to participate in various games or events: *toros de soga*, *ensogado*, *maroma*, *atados*. Goya depicted one bull tied by the horns in this way, which might show that the animal had been captured with the lasso, since the scene is thought to be a hunt.

Several travellers did not regard the 'bull games' they witnessed in South America as Spanish *corridas*. In Quito in 1876 the spectacle was described as 'innocent bull-running': 'Nowhere in America are there to be found any true bullfights, unless it is in Lima'.[12] In 1869 it was reckoned that 'the art of bullfighting is still in its infancy in Cuzco'.[13] In Venezuela bullfighting differed from the Spanish sport on two counts: the bull was from a poor breed and more than half dazed by the beating it had received in the bullpen while having its horns shaved: the entire bullfight involved 'sticking *banderillas de fuego*' into the

G. Batta Molinelli, *Panorama of Lima*, c. 1680, colour lithograph.

bull. In 1929 in San Vitorino, Colombia, one traveller wrote that 'it cannot be called a fight', likening it to a show of *Gineta*-style horsemanship instead.[14] At a festival held in a Colombian mountain village (San Cristobal Potreros) in 1888, the *rejóneadors* were seen to wound the animal without killing it.[15] In Jalapa, William Bullock saw a 'mimic kind' of bullfight.[16] These travellers gave no information about the injuries inflicted on the animal, or its killing, which did not seem to be par for the course. The bull was provoked by injuries inflicted with various harpoons, as in the present-day *corralejas* (amateur bullfights). In other places, there were identifiable *capeas* and mounted bullfights.

Although swept along by the atmosphere at these spectacles, which were not always cruel or bloodthirsty and were often attended by a colourful crowd taking part in an exuberant carnival, these travellers were still shocked by several specific events. In Lima in 1843 the spectators revolted because of an uncooperative bull. They invaded the ring and 'by tormenting these unfortunate animals . . . [they finally] achieved the desired result . . . the death of two or three Indians'.[17] Fighting between a bull, tiger or dogs incensed them as much as cockfighting and the goring of horses in bullfights. Henri de Saussure wrote 'after the bull had been thoroughly tortured, the matador arrived'. He recounted the anecdote of a father comforting his son at one such event: 'There weren't any accidents, today . . . but there will be next time, I promise'.[18] Finally, 'You have to have been born Spanish to take the slightest pleasure in a series of scenes that are so cruel and revolting', or again, 'They were trying to make a peaceable animal vicious and they were accustoming people to the sight of bloodshed, when they need to be pacified by moving scenes'.[19]

Marchioness Fanny de Calderon reiterated Goya's exclamation *barbara diversion* and described a bull 'beside itself with pain, leaking blood, bristling with *banderillas* and covered with fireworks'.[20] Except in Lima, where they attended the bullring, travellers tended to prefer rural celebrations. Closer to the action than in the large bullrings, and less influenced by the press, these visitors condemned the cruelties they saw, but without describing the killing in detail.

In the eighteenth century there were far more travellers in the Iberian peninsula than in South America and their published accounts circulated in Europe in translation. Nearly all these books, which were helpful to manufacturers who were exporting to South America via Cadiz, devoted a chapter to the inevitable bullfight their authors claimed to have seen, if possible embellished with dramatic incidents.[21] Every country produced its own literature, Spain less than others, due to censorship. In actual fact, *Les Délices d'Espagne et du Portugal* by Alvarez de Colmenar, published in Leiden in 1715 and condemned by the Inquisition (1747), criticized royal bullfights with their 'bloody combats' for being wasteful and at odds with the 'rules of Christianity'. The later *Carta Historica* (1777) on the origins of bullfighting in Spain by Nicolas-Fernandez de Moratín, commissioned by Pignatelli, minister of King Ferdinand IV, put forward a whimsical explanation of the origins of the bullfight, whose cruelty he attributed to the Moors who, under Spain's civilizing influence, were 'forsaking the superstitions of the Koran'. Conquerors of bulls included the legendary figures of Charles V and El Cid. Goya's borrowings from Moratín, inserted among the engravings of the *Tauromaquia* at a later date, are surprising; his friend Vargas de Ponce criticized Moratín for being an *aficionado*. However, the

Francisco Goya, *Charles V Spearing a Bull in the Ring at Valladolid*, preparatory red chalk drawing for *Tauromaquia*.

elderly Goya was in occasional contact with Moratin's son, Leandro. One of Europe's best-sellers was written by an Englishman, Edward Clarke, a 'Fellow at St John's College, Cambridge'. He accompanied Sir George Williams, Earl of Bristol, and English ambassador in Spain, to the celebrations of sovereignty held in 1760 in honour of Charles III.

Several English writers described bullfighting: Richard Twiss, a virtuoso musician, in Santa-Maria, 1771;[22] soldiers like William Dalrymple in Córdoba, 1774;[23] Richard Crocker in Arcos de la Frontera, 1780;[24] Joseph Townsend, a Pastor, in Madrid, 1791;[25] and the plutocrat William Beckford.[26] There was a trio of French diplomats, Étienne de Silhouette; Jean François Peyron;[27] and his friend Jean-François Bourgoing, who denounced the Inquisition and bullfighting, and whose book was as widely distributed as Clarke's work. The Franco-Italian archaeologist Henri Swinburne from Havana witnessed bull-fights in Córdoba and Aranjuez (1776).[28] Various Mediterranean travellers criticized bullfighting: Norbert Caimo;[29] Barnabite (a bullfight in Aranjuez, 1755); and Baretti (bullfight in Lisbon, 1760).[30] German travellers included Peter Löfling, a Linnean disciple, who described his dual expe-dition to Spain and America (1751).[31]

On 16 July 1760 Edward Clarke watched a majestic spectacle from the terraces of the Plaza

A. B., *Torero on Horseback*, 1855, lithograph.

Mayor in Madrid. Formerly employed in the hunt, *lanzadas*, which involved impaling the bull on a row of lances, were used in conjunction with bullfighting methods. Horses spilled their guts on the ground, *banderillas de fuego* exploded in wounds, watchdogs tore the bulls limb from limb, and bullfighters on foot finished off the victims, cutting and thrusting with their swords. Clarke, invited as a member of the diplomatic corps, obviously had to be somewhat restrained in his description.[32] Clarke was one of the first to defend violence at these festivals:

This spectacle is certainly one of the finest in the world, whether it is considered merely as a *coup d'oeil*, or as an exertion of the bravery and infinite agility of the performers . . . There is a certain degree of ferocity requisite in our natures; and which, as on the one hand, it should be restrained within proper bounds, that it may not degenerate into cruelty; so, on the other, we must not refine too much upon it, for fear of sinking into effeminacy. This custom is far from having cruelty for its object; bravery and intrepidity, joined with ability and skill, are what obtain the loudest acclamations from the people.

Clarke did not deny that the spectacle was cruel, but he believed it useful for men. He skilfully disseminated the military paradox: there is nothing cruel about torture if the torturer takes no pleasure in it and has a laudable motive, if he is killing an enemy or merely doing it for reasons of war. Bullfighting, like war, strengthened male virility. His argument, which was well expressed, became the *leitmotiv* for the opponents of animal rights, when there were demands for animal protection in British politics. From the early nineteenth century, anti-slavery campaigners endeavoured to obtain a ban on bull-baiting in Britain, continually opposed by the War Minister, William Windham.

William Beckford,[33] future Lord of Fonthill, regarded animals as superior brothers; he was infuriated by Portuguese bullfighting: 'and though scared with fireworks, pricked with swords, worried by dogs, and provoked by the grinning negros, [the bulls] never ventured to attack the horseman. It requires little courage to attack such patient animals . . . I seemed to feel cuts and slashes the rest of the evening'.[34] The German botanist Friedrich Link remarked on the working-class audience, and the presence of women, in a wooden bullring. Riders armed with lances fought bulls with sheathed horns, which were not very aggressive; they tortured a calf, 'It is a dismal sport. There is nothing beautiful about this fight'.[35]

An Italian scholar, Giuseppe Baretti,[36] proved that not everyone from Mediterranean countries were *aficionados*. In August 1760 he attended a bullfighting festival in Campo Pequeno, an octagonal wooden amphitheatre located at the time on the outskirts of Lisbon, and 'erected for the only purpose of exhibiting these barbarous entertainments . . . [A bull received] such a cut on the back between the ribs, as almost cleft him to the middle . . . Eighteen were the bulls slaughtered in this feast of hunting, and each with some variety of wanton cruelty.'

The French were even more indignant. 'Everything appals here', wrote the journalist Fleuriot de Langle about bullfighting. His *Voyage de Figaro en Espagne* drew its inspiration from Beaumarchais.[37] The author, a journalist, attacked Spanish social and political abuses and the Inquisition. He denounced the suffering of animals and the death penalty for human beings and animals, without wasting any time on the technicalities of bullfighting, about which he knew very little. Charles III commissioned a *Dénonciation au public du voyage d'un soi-disant Figaro en Espagne par le véritable Figaro* (London, 1785) from the Count of Aranda, who provided information about the physical cruelty inflicted on the bull before the bullfight (stabbing, turpentine on the hooves), but added the eternal refrain: 'Whoever defends animals professes himself to be man's enemy.' The French

Mules in the Plaza de Toros, Madrid.

courts sentenced Fleuriot's *Voyage de Figaro* to a ridiculous book-burning in a public square, which created a great deal of publicity for the work, translated into English, Danish, German and Italian.[38]

Jean-Jacques Rousseau, one of the earliest champions of animal rights, mentioned bullfighting in his *Considérations sur le gouvernement de Pologne*. 'Look at Spain, where the bullfights have done much to keep a certain vigour alive in the people.' Rousseau suggested an alternative in the handling of horses: 'Nothing would be easier than to work out, instead of the fights for which the circuses were customarily used, competitions that would be less cruel in character, yet would call for strength and skill'. Jean-Luc Guichet believes that Rousseau admitted the value of an as yet unidentified sport in providing warrior training and that he 'was distancing himself by showing that these constructive effects could be achieved by more humane methods, far more in keeping with his overall philosophy'.[39]

Erudite travellers rarely mentioned bullfighting, which did not appear in the books by the English agriculturalist Arthur Young or those by archaeologists and scientists. However, most accounts of bullfighting (and not the celebrations of sovereignty approved by Clarke) used language that exuded indignation in English, German, Italian and Spanish, for example:

'torturing a poor unfortunate bull';[40] bulls 'cruelly tormented';[41] 'bulls dying in horrible agony';[42] 'appalling entertainment';[43] 'a vulgar spectacle which dishonours humanity';[44] 'pitilessly sacrificing innocent animals';[45] 'dismal sport'.[46] Goya's expression *Barbara diversion* joined forces with Baretti's 'barbarous entertainments'.[47] Jean-François Bourgoing, having declared that neither bullfighting nor the Inquisition ought 'to have any apologists but executioners', added:

> With these spectators disgust succeeds to compassion and ennui to disgust . . . It will be believed with difficulty that the art of killing a bull, which seems to be the exclusively the business of a butcher, should be gravely discussed, and exalted with transport, not only by the people, but by men of sense, by women of delicacy.[48]

The French explorer and photographer Désiré Charnay reported that the bullfight had undergone a terrible transposition, featuring men rather than bulls. During their national festivities, the rebel Indians of Santa Cruz were executing their prisoners: 'With a ring through their nose, they were made to play the part of the bull in an arena . . . pursued with stones, arrows and lances, they breathed their last in nameless torment, they were not left alone until their body, forming nothing more than an open wound, collapsed in pain and exhaustion'.[49] By shifting the cruelty inflicted on

CORRIDA DE TOROS
GUERRITA DESCABELLANDO

The bullring, Madrid, in a postcard sent New Year's Day 1900.

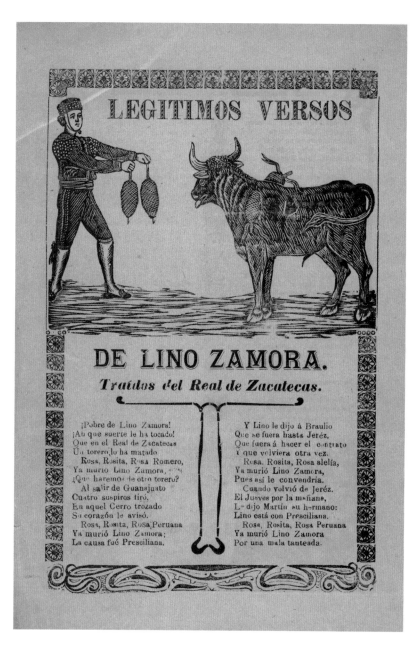

Legitimos Versos: Mexican bullfighting handbill, c. 1910.

the bulls in the *corrida* onto the men they hated, the Indians showed they were fully aware of the inhumane barbarity of bullfighting, denounced by the majority of travellers in Spain and Latin America in the eighteenth century. It would not be long before a discourse emerged that began to convince *aficionados*, concerned by their attraction for such 'fascinating atrocities', that refusing to watch was proof of superior intellectual faculties.

five

Nineteenth-century Spain and Latin America

French Romantic literature played a key role in the spread of bullfighting beyond Spain. France's ruling house was in fact linked to Spanish royalty. In 1846 Philippe d'Orléans, son of King Louis-Philippe, married the sister of Queen Isabella II. His court and the 'Jeune France' group took up residence in Seville in 1848.

A dazzling array of talents wrote accounts of bullfighting. The fashion for Romantic 'fascinating atrocities' both vindicated and reassured the Spanish. After the shock of the French Revolution, returning emigrants, having survived the Terror and the subsequent wars, attempted to ease their malaise by sublimating the horror, an act that Joseph de Maistre transformed into the cult of redemptive suffering.[1]

Melodrama was the keynote of both literature and the plays performed on the Parisian boulevards. The young Prosper Mérimée wrote incessantly about murders and massacres. Beyond the distressing sight of a decaying carcass, Baudelaire described the pleasure afforded by torture: 'Victims in tears, the hangman glorified, / The banquet seasoned and festooned with blood'.[2] Beneath his apparent terror, he savoured the enjoyment of extreme, forbidden emotions.[3] In France, the military and royalist backing for Ferdinand VII, which incensed liberals, caused a wave of support for provincial Spain. Mérimée's *Théâtre de Clara Gazul*, followed quickly by Victor Hugo and many others, created a lasting fashion.

In 1830 in Spain Mérimée met the influential Montijo family (one daughter, Eugenia, married Napoleon), who introduced him to the *corrida*. Back in France, Mérimée became the champion of bullfighting, and his account, published in the *Revue de Paris*, introduced the deathless justification of an indomitable passion for bullfighting, indistinguishable from a glorification of war which, 'with all its horrors, has extraordinary charms'. He thought the *banderillas de fuego* were an 'admirable sight', as was the bull 'shaking the flaming sticks, and tossing amid fire and smoke': the rabble laughed, and the writer was full of admiration, Praising bullfighting also pleased the Empress. In his *Voyage en Espagne* (1843), Théophile Gautier feigned pity for the bull, while Alexandre Dumas, in *De Paris à Cadix* (1846), dramatized the spectacle: fear caused the spectators to wallow in delicious anxiety, and bullfighting acquired the same appeal as a public execution. From 1845 Carmen became the ubiquitous ambassadress for bullfighting, while waiting to mount the opera stage.

These three legendary writings served as international source material until the twentieth century. The homage paid by the German poet Rainer Maria Rilke to the matador Montes

Francisco Montes (1804–51),
c. 1836, a print of the famous
bullfighter who introduced the
'suit of lights' (*traje de luz*) into
the ring.

Gustave Doré, *Fall of a Picador*,
c. 1860, colour lithograph.

owed everything to Gautier, as reinterpreted by the painter Zuloaga, and nothing to reality. In fact, Rilke stayed in a bad hotel in Ronda, about which he complained, and he did not even visit the bullring. Contradictorily, throughout his work, he devoted 'the ideal of intransitive love' to the 'living and all the world . . .'.[4] In July 1809, at the age of 21, Byron, a member of the House of Lords with a reputation for licentiousness, set off with his friend Hobhouse to visit the Mediterranean.[5] Soon after his return in 1811 Byron published the first two cantos of *Childe Harold's Pilgrimage*, a narrative poem recounting their trip, which included eight stanzas on a bullfight in Andalucia. It is easy in these lines to identify the *Tercios*, the *muleta*, which became a red cloak, and the *banderillas*, which looked like 'darts'. The stakes of a battle like this, as dangerous as a jousting tournament, and the sight of manly courage, arouse women's admiration. The bull is a fierce, mighty, foaming brute. 'Red rolls his eye's dilated glow' as the beast charges at the familiar steed, which is gored: 'hideous sight'! 'Dart follows dart; lance, lance'; the bull falls amidst triumphant cries, without a groan or struggle.

Everything was swept away by this gamut of violent emotions, and Byron was fascinated. The success of *Childe Harold's Pilgrimage* firmly established Byron in literary society and conferred an aesthetic status on bullfighting. Whether deliberately or not, Byron had transformed killing into an alluring saga cited by *aficionados*, but also by an American opponent of bullfighting, John A. Dix:

> Such the ungentle sport that oft invites
> The Spanish maid and cheers the Spanish
>   swain

> Nurtured in blood betimes, his heart delights
> In vengeance, gloating on another's pain
> What private feuds the troubled village stain
> Though now one phalanxed host should
>   meet the foe
> Enough, alas! in humble homes remain
> To meditate 'gainst friend the secret blow
> For some slight cause of wrath, whence life's
>   warm stream must flow'.[6]

During Europe's infatuation with Spain, the British capital welcomed numerous Spanish emigrants, and a Spanish chair was created at the University of London. Henry Richard, a leading promoter of Spanish culture and of prints produced in Britain that illustrated bullfighting, struck up a friendship with Jovellanos. The number of travel books escalated after the Napoleonic blockade had ended. One by Thomas Roscoe,[7] distributed in Philadelphia, was very popular with its gilded edges and its engraved illustrations by David Roberts, including the frontispiece depicting the *Bullring of Seville*. This work included a detailed history of bullfighting and its successive and recent bans, as well as the death of Pepe-Hillo. Roscoe believed that all types of fighting, including bullfighting, were 'all branches from the same stem', from the gladiators to the English prize-ring. In chapter Six he transcribed some passages from Byron, and it was not long before he too attracted a following.

THE ENGLISH IN MEXICO CITY

Humboldt's *Political Essay on the Kingdom of New Spain* came out in London in 1811, after being published in Paris (1808). Despite three revolutions in Mexico (1820, 1830 and 1848), Mexico City represented an attractive commercial outlet for the British.[8] Imposing and picturesque,

James Gillray, *The Spanish Bull-fight or the Corsican Matador in Danger*, 1808, etching.

the rural and urban landscapes invited international scholars and artists, some of whom settled there. Native festivals rivalled the bullfighting spectacles. Nevertheless, the Swiss artist J. S. Hegi depicted a *torero* in Spanish-style dress, with a *rejóneador*. The renowned genre painter and prolific illustrator Juan Mauricio Rugendas, a Catalan artist exiled to Augsburg who then settled in Mexico City, depicted a bullfighting poster in the square at Lima, although he hardly ever painted the bullring. Baron Gros, son of a successful French painter, produced albums of drawings of Mexico City with the Baron de Courcy. When it came to English artists, the

watercolours by the traveller George Henry White or the engravings by Daniel Thomas Egerton and many others provided information about Mexican treasures, landscapes, monuments and human types. Hubert Sattler from Salzburg, among other entrepreneurs, travelled all over America, capturing surprising aspects of the landscape, as in his *Total View of Mexico* City (1854).

William Bullock, a jeweller from Liverpool, was one of the first merchants in regular contact with Mexico City. Famous for his exotic gallery of natural history in London, he exhibited curious objects like the coach Napoleon used on the occasion of the Battle of Waterloo, and he also organized a Mexican museum. He published *Six Months' Residence and Travels in Mexico*, 'containing remarks on the present state of New Spain, its natural productions, state of society, manufactures, trade, agriculture, and antiquities', with maps.[9] His impressive reconstructions and his concepts of an ideal city (Hygeia) were reminiscent of Barnum. In Jalapa, he attended a bullfight: 'It was the first time I had witnessed any thing like a bull-fight . . . and as the parties did not seem to apprehend any peril, the laughter, in which the females had not inconsiderable share, was occasionally very boisterous and long-continued'. In 1823, when Mexico achieved independence, Bullock gave a panoramic sketch to the painter Burford, who made a panorama for London's Leicester Square, described in several advertisements.[10] This panorama showed an enclosed arena, erected in front of the Mexican Palacio, the El Volador market, San Agustin Street, the parliament building and the 34 arcades around the square. An Englishman who had read Roscoe and Byron, and had then seen the panorama, might have been forgiven for thinking that bullfighting was a time-honoured spectacle, a courtly epic, and that there was a bullring at the centre of one of the most remarkable cities in the world. These misconceptions, however, did not prevent the law of 18 June 1833 being passed in London. This law, the first worldwide legislation for the protection of fighting bulls, prohibited people from keeping these animals.[11] This victory by animal protectors, assisted by opponents of slavery like William Wilberforce, was wrung from the House of Lords after a 30-year-long fight that had originally been initiated to outlaw bull-baiting.

Skeleton bullfighter toy for the Mexican 'Day of the Dead'.

Mexico City, which was close to various ranches, organized bullfighting festivals to take place on specially adapted squares. These bullfights, which charged an admission fee, brought in a substantial revenue. The main season at the Plaza del Volador of 1770 brought in around 40,000 *pesos*,[12] which were earmarked for the Alamedo promenade or the Chapultepec Palace, major colonialist haunts. Bullfighting festivities included novelty pieces (*mojigangas*), mounted bullfighting and bulls bearing fireworks (*enmantados de cohetes y fuegos*), as depicted on an eighteenth-century triumphal arch. They provided a forum for the Indians' skilled horsemanship. José Joaquín Fernández de Lizardi denounced these spectacles as a 'bloody diversion . . . for making hearts savage and eliminating any notion of sensitivity in humble men'. A radical opponent with deep sympathy for Enlightenment thought, Lizardi invented an anti-bullfighting dialogue between a bull and a horse.[13]

In 1788 one of the town's unions denounced the harmful effects of the recurrent festivals: workers were striking to force their employers to give them free admission tickets. None of the viceroys in Mexico City was an *aficionado*, except Bernardo de Galvez. They either reduced the number of bullfights being held or banned them altogether. Marquina cancelled the bullfighting festival organized for his grand entry, covering the costs himself. In 1805, the ban by Charles IV was enforced on a long-term basis in Mexico City, even though Father Michel Hidalgo, who had a vested interest in bullfighting since he owned three ranches in Michoacan, was gracing the bullfights with his presence.[14] The liberal reforms of Cadiz (1812) were celebrated without bullfights; some separatist Creoles founded a democratic municipality,[15] which was silenced by Fernando VII.

In 1814 there were joint celebrations for the return of absolute power, the Inquisition and bullfighting. The wooden structures from the Plaza del Volador, with their free seats, were set up in the Plaza San Pablo, where the permanent arena became a symbol of absolute Spanish power; the revenue from bullfighting was used to maintain the army. If the arena in the Leicester Square Panorama could have been identified as the San Pablo bullring, it would have represented the temple of loathed Spanish absolutism. In 1821 the entry of the people's idol, General Agustín de Iturbide, into Mexico City marked a break with Spain, which verged on hatred: Cortes's remains were saved with difficulty, and bullfighting temporarily became a symbol of the former Iberian oppressor.

GOYA'S 'BARBAROUS PASTIME'

Goya witnessed the birth of bullfighting and with his youthful companions in Aragon probably enjoyed bullfights, but his correspondence with his childhood friend, Martin Zapater reveals that his true passion was for hunting with a gun, since he talked tirelessly about his exploits as a celebrated shot. In thirty years of correspondence with Zapater, bullfighting was only mentioned briefly on three occasions (7 October 1775; 7 January 1794; 24 April 1794) as well as in a few later comments to Leandro Moratín (7 October 1825).

Goya was commissioned to produce a tapestry cartoon, the *Novillada*, which formed part of a sequence devoted to popular life. On close inspection it is possible to make out an atypical self-portrait. The artist painted the portrait of the matador Pedro Romero (1795–8), but in Sanlucar de Barrameda, at the house of the Duchess of Alba, who was a keen *aficionada*, there are very few drawings of bulls among the 500 surviving pictures. Goya painted portraits of many bull-fighting opponents – the king, Godoy, his great friend Melchor de Jovellanos. The artist wrote *Barbara diversion* in pencil on the first plate of the copy of the *Tauromaquia* owned by Céan Bermúdez, his friend, a salesman. This priceless treasure was bought and examined by the London antiques dealer Tomás Harris, who gifted it to the British Museum in London.

Barbara ('barbarous') was a word repeatedly used to describe bullfighting in the eighteenth century, particularly by Vargas Ponce.[16] Goya's pencil inscription, which was to remain unknown for a century and a half, was first published around 1980.[17] In 2001 the *Tauromaquia* exhibition at the Print Room of the Prado Museum

in Madrid, with its splendid catalogue, provided fresh insight into this series, engraved by Goya in 1815.[18] The red chalk drawings are sketches for copperplate engravings. Tomás Harris studied the plates, the paper, the watermarks, the different techniques and states; in this way he restored the sequence in which the engravings were undertaken, the earliest being made not long after the *Executions of the 3 May in La Moncloa* and very close in time to the *Disasters of War* (not published until 1868). Other researchers closely examined the texts, their variations, and their sources, which had until then been restricted to Moratín, thereby revealing the influence of Vargas Ponce. Thirteen of Goya's plates were directly inspired by his texts. Moratín's *Carta Historica* was one of the first whimsical stories (1777) in favour of bullfighting. The use of these pseudo-historic themes,

Goya's annotations to a bound volume of working proofs of *Tauromaquia* presented to his friend Céan Bermúdez.

Francisco Goya, *Dreadful Events in the Front Rows of the Ring at Madrid and the Death of the Mayor of Torrejón*, preparatory red chalk drawing for *Tauromaquia*.

Francisco Goya, *The Charge of the Powerful Bull*, preparatory red chalk drawing for *Tauromaquia*.

featuring Charles v or El Cid, endeavoured to ennoble and vindicate bullfighting, which was coming under a great deal of criticism. It was thought that Céan Bermúdez might have advised Goya to turn to Moratín in a bid to make the *Tauromaquia* more marketable. Apart from the 'diversions' (*mojigangas*), Goya depicted

acrobatics, Apinani's famous pole vault and the challenge by his friend, Martincho. Not many of the scenes in the first editions (34 plates) were devoted to the three *Tercios*, but there were more later in the posthumous editions.

In his *Tauromaquia*, Goya highlighted the inhumanity of bullfighting by the simplest of

Francisco Goya, 'The Agility and Audacity of Juanito Apiñani in the Ring at Madrid', from *Tauromaquia*, 1816, engraving.

Francisco Goya, 'They Loose Dogs on the Bull', preparatory red chalk drawing for *Tauromaquia*.

Francisco Goya, 'Manly Courage of the Celebrated Pajuelera in the Ring at Zaragoza', from *Tauromaquia*, 1816, engraving.

Francisco Goya, 'The same [Mariano] Ceballos, Mounted on a Bull, breaks Short Spears in the Ring at Madrid', from *Tauromaquia*, 1816, engraving.

methods – the only tools needed by a great talent. A shaft of light or an impression of latency were enough to create the sense of drama inherent in the space between the lethal point and the animal's flesh, whether dart or *rejón*, the curved blade of the *media luna*, or the dagger held by the Indian straddling a bull. The red chalk drawings, which are even more lifelike than their copperplate counterparts, have little in common with the technical nature of the most skilful commercial

Francisco Goya,
Bullfight, Suerte de Varas, 1824,
oil on canvas.

Francisco Goya, 'Bullfight
in a Divided Ring', from
Bulls of Bordeaux, 1825,
lithograph.

engravings. In them Goya depicted a bloody drama, whereas Carnicero maintained a cooler, more technical focus.

What Vargas Ponce expressed through words, Goya showed through images. He detected (rather than denounced) man's debasement in his enjoyment of the suffering inflicted on animals. As in his *Caprices*, Goya merely makes the hidden violence visible. He reveals the violence that is concealed by social convention or financial interests.

Philippe Louis Parizeau (1740–1801), *Bull Killing its Fifth Horse in the Ring*, aquatint.

The *Caprices* tackled the violence inflicted by men on women, by adults on children, and by superstitions on the gullible; the *Disasters of War* showed the violence inflicted on the population by war; and the *Tauromaquia* revealed man's violence towards animals. It is not surprising that Mérimée did not understand Goya at all: he felt that Goya 'couldn't even draw bulls properly'.[19]

Despite the historical pretext provided by Moratín, the *Tauromaquia* sold so badly that Goya advised the publishers to drop the price. The painter's situation was dire. He lost his wife, then his patrons, Charles IV and Godoy, while his friends, Jovellanos and Bermúdez, had drifted

away. Even worse, after the French invasion of Spain, his faith in the culture of the Enlightenment had crumbled. In Bordeaux, where Goya had taken up residence, the printer Gaulon introduced him to lithography, a printmaking technique that is closer to drawing. The *Diversión de España* was aimed at Spanish emigrants. Once again, it depicted the *jaripeo* put on by Mariano Ceballos. The shared arena showed spectators invading the bullring in rustic fashion.[20] The draughtsmanship is still dazzling and has lost none of its power.

Goya's *Tauromaquia* was a work of universal significance, but it made no impact on the bullfighting world of his time. It was rediscovered in France under the Second Empire, then republished and consistently interpreted as the work of an *aficionado*, without any serious examination; as far as these superficial exegetes were concerned, any representation amounted to approval and, even worse, justification for the subject depicted. The small bullfighting paintings, on copper, which showed scenes from *corridas*, depicted a series of typical institutions (around 1792), such as prisons for the insane, *autos-da-fé*, and processions. Authenticated bullfighting paintings by Goya, like *Les Piques* (for Ferrer, Paris, 1824), are rare, because Eugenio Lucas Velázquez (1817–1870) became Goya's regular plagiarist and his son may also have painted for Manet.

THE END OF THE CELEBRITY MATADORS

Following the death of Pepe-Hillo (1801) and the Spanish War of Independence (1808–14), the celebrity matadors disappeared. After bullfighting had been reinstated by José Bonaparte, in 1814 Ferdinand VII closed the universities and opened a bullfighting school, politicizing bullfighting. Isabella II invited 'warriors to the best-loved spectacle of the Spanish'. In this favourable climate, Francisco Montes Reina (1805–1851) learned the profession, taking advantage of the royal bullfighting school in Seville and the advice he was given by the elderly Pedro Romero. Blessed with a pronounced sense of theatre, this consummate athlete livened up the bullring with his nimble agility, so different from the outmoded formality of bullfighting in Ronda. He invented dramatic poses, for example presenting his back to the bull (*gallear el toro*) and making the animal, which was fairly small at that time (1.4 metres), pass under his arm. He also restored discipline to the *cuadrilla*. One

Francisco Montes, c. 1836, lithograph.

traveller, John A. Dix, saw Montes performing around 1843.[21] After the *banderilleros* came in, it was 'the last stage of torture', as a trumpet sounded. Dix described an *estocada a recibir* by Montes, dressed 'in a richly embroidered jacket', 'pointing . . . the fatal sword at the bull's neck'. He then went on to describe the spectacle: 'loathsome, disgusting, brutal and barbarous – a scene only fit to gratify assassins and to create them – managed with some dexterity, it is true, but without a particle of chivalric bearing and under all its aspects, a stain upon the humanity and the civilisation of the age'. Talking about war, Dix added that 'the cruelty with which the civil wars of Spain have been waged of late years – the

A 19th-century lithograph by 'G.D.' and 'E.D.', showing *forcados* immobilizing a bull.

hands cut off, the eyes put out, the horrible maimings, in modes too wanton and loathsome to be named – are all the legitimate offspring of the lessons of barbarity taught in the arena'.

In 1836 Montes, a worthy successor to Pepe-Hillo, wrote a practical manual.[22] He modified the lance, and invented or named some cape passes, including the famous *veronica*, in memory of the saint who imprinted Christ's blood-streaked face on a piece of fabric. A brilliant advertising agent, Santos López Pelegrín, known as Abenamar, prepared Montes's treatise for publication and alerted the press, *El Mundo*, then *El Correo Nacional* (1838). He became the first professional impresario who was in business to make a profit. A precursor of the intellectual wandering minstrel, Pelegrín published a *Filosofía de Los Toros* (1842). This informed readers that the horse was proud to die on the bullfight's field of honour, that those against bullfighting were cowardly draft-

dodgers, that violence was justified by 'universal barbarity' and, therefore, by itself, which is only too true.

Montes, a skilful performer in the bullring, then made it his mission to enhance the dramatic appearance of the matador's costume, assisted by a dressmaker, Amalia Manfredi. Mérimée claimed that Montes drew his inspiration from Figaro's outfit in *The Barber of Seville*. In contrast, the *alguacillo* (mounted constable) retained the understated costume of the seventeenth-century gentleman. The matador's shortened jacket (*chaquetilla*) was heavily covered with gold, which was particularly eye-catching during the *paseo* (parade) around 5 pm. The very heavy braid, which resembled wall hangings when seen up close, made the suit sparkle from a distance. The extravagant appearance of the Romantic costume was its main advantage. The so-called 'suit of lights' played down the role of the killer,

Giuseppe Signore, c. 1875, watercolour drawing of a picador.

Luigi Lablache in the role of Figaro in *The Barber of Seville*, Vienna, 1820, polychrome lithograph.

matador in Spanish, which is the title role of the bullfight.

It was therefore with good reason that Coluche wrote that 'in Spain, the butcher is smartly dressed'.[23] An aphorism about the function of the costume uses a similar process: 'Members of the Jury, I have put on gloves to kill, so I am not a murderer, but a dandy.'

If transcribed for bullfighting, this phrase might run: 'Spectators, I have put on my suit of lights to kill, so I am not a killer, I am an artist.' The author of this strangely irresponsible statement was the writer and *aficionado* Jean Cau, who also ridiculed opponents of the death penalty in his book.[24] Elias Canetti meditated in great depth on the masking function of any uniform worn for killing: 'If you all had to face one another naked, you would have a hard time slaughtering. The murderous uniforms!'[25] George Bernard Shaw observed that 'All dress is fancy dress, is it not, except our natural skins?'[26] The uniform distances the murderer from his act, shifting the responsibility onto the remote creator of the suit. In bullfighting, the suit of lights transforms the bullring into a theatre, and the animal's real suffering into fiction. Once he was cured of his *afición*, Leiris came up with a formula that could be applied to the suit of lights: 'a hideous reverse linked to a glittering obverse'.[27]

However, the new style of Spanish *corrida* did not win over the Portuguese. In 1836 the Brazilian-born Queen Maria de la Gloria denounced what for her was a 'barbarous spectacle unworthy of civilized nations'. She banned killing in the bullring and insisted that protective spheres were placed on the bull's horns. As always, the political argument – the secular opposition between Portugal and Spain – took precedence over any sympathy for the animals.[28]

A rustic *suerte* or act then gained a certain degree of popularity with tourists: *pegadores* or *mozos de forcado*, unarmed participants wearing red and green pointed hats, immobilized the bull, already bristling with *banderillas*, by seizing it by the horns and tail. In Portugal, the spectators enjoyed displays of horsemanship. The *rejón* wielded by riders, who were often stoutly built

'Passes with the Cape', lithograph in José Velazquez y Sanchez, *Anales del Toreo* (1868).

The vest of a matador.

(to withstand the impact) and wearing eighteenth-century courtly costumes, killed the bulls by impaling them alive. Photographs taken in 1988 show a bull pierced from side to side by formidable steel points. As was the case everywhere, it was stated that the bull was 'brave and impassive in vain'; it is provoked by the lances and 'injuries are necessary . . . to enrage the bull', otherwise it will 'stop and run away'.[29]

SOUTH AMERICA AND THE *CORRIDAS*

After bullfighting spectacles were prohibited in Argentina in 1822, Chile passed a radical perma-nent ban: at the same time, in 1823, General Bernardo O'Higgins abolished slavery, bull-fighting and cockfighting. These men of Spanish descent objected to 'horrific spectacles fit for barbarous times that debase the spectators, the *lidia de toros*'.[30] By acknowledging human dignity and animal sensibility, they heralded a new type of relationship between men and animals. A few of the victorious generals in Latin America were sons of the Enlightenment, and opposed to the degrading, cruel exploitation of animals for entertainment. The prohibition of bullfighting in 1823 in Chile marked a watershed in the history of animal rights. One year after Martin's Act was passed in Britain, it proved that neither cruelty to animals nor bullfighting were deeply rooted in man's character or in human civilization. However, it would take the work of several generations to make the rejection of bullfighting a simple fact. In legal matters, Bolivia, which was flourishing around 1834, adopted the Napoleonic mindset and penal code, as characterized by its reactionary reification of animals.

From 20 June 1810 (the independence of Colombia) and 1811 (independence celebrations in Venezuela) to 1821 (independence of Mexico) and the independence celebrations in Peru (28 July 1821), colonial ties were broken with Spain in all Latin American bullfighting countries. However, hatred of the Spanish did not inevitably go hand in hand with a rejection of bullfighting and cruelty towards animals continued to exert a fascination.

Around 1825 South America was decimated, soldiers went unpaid and the officers were continually changed. Argentina and Gran Colombia rose up. Taking advantage of the widespread discord, various dictators seized power for many years in Venezuela and Ecuador.[31] In the former Spanish colonies 'colonial ties had been broken, but colonialism continued . . . it had become internal.'[32] Against this backdrop, skilled Creole or Spanish traders finally succeeded in exploiting bullfighting. In 1834, Spaniards from Navarre, wealthy inhabitants of Lima, bought the ranch of Rinconada de Mala, which was to supply the bullring at Acho in Lima with bulls for as many as five bullfights per year.[33]

In 1821 in Venezuela some speculators invested in plans for bullrings and a corporation of breeders was formed that sent bulls to the spectacles. In Ecuador, the Ganadería de Pedregal seemed to be continuing the tradition of the Jesuits' small Navarre bulls. They provided cattle for the highly original 'bull games' described by Stevenson before 1830, in which the bulls were neither killed nor too badly injured.[34] Stevenson provided an amusing description of a festival on a square equipped for a large-scale carnival, with permission from the President. All social classes rubbed shoulders. The participants entered the bullring together from all four corners of the enclosure, and paraded in their thousands for an hour; many joined the spectators and greeted them; musicians and torch-bearers, sellers of cold drinks, and supervisors kept order among the people wearing masks. It was forbidden to pull off the masks (made in Quito), which represented local figures. If anyone did, 'monkeys . . . would flog the aggressor with their long tails, the friars would strike with their beads, and the muleteers with their whips'. Bulls made their way through the crowd, which formed a tight 'wall of bellies', as the bulls tried to find a way out. The *aficionados*, either on foot or on horseback, provoked the bulls to charge, probably by injuring them. They changed the tired beasts and the festival continued.

The strong military presence in the bullrings, particularly in Peru, seemed typical of South America. In Lima's Acho bullring in around 1800 the soldiers sat on reserved seats, with their rifles between their legs,[35] or paraded to music. They annoyed the spectators, who were crying '*toros*'. The troops occasionally intervened to empty the bullring of angry spectators, but in the main the soldiers seemed to be deeply appreciated as protectors.[36] In Cuzco in Peru, soldiers wearing uniforms, which attracted admiration, behaved very strangely; when they departed, they left the words *viva el Peru* spelled out in rose petals on the sand![37] The troops were sometimes paid to provide music for the spectacles; in Mexico (Paseo Nuevo) in 1862 this budget accounted for 0.75 per cent of the overall expenditure.

six

Bullfighting, Art, Opera and Dance

By the mid-nineteenth century in South America, bullfighting had cast off its detested associations with the imperial power of Spain. In Mexico City, Bartolome Jiménez founded a school of Mexican-style bullfighting, while its inhabitants continued to impale the bulls on lances on the square in Maravetio Grande.[1] The Spanish *torero*, Bernardo Gaviño (born 1813), settled in Mexico City in 1835 and trained Ponciano Díaz (born 1858). However, the Plaza de Toros del Paseo Nuevo, built in 1851, was demolished as a result of the ban in 1867, and there continued to be strong opposition to bullfighting. The Marquise Calderón de la Barca, wife of the first United States ambassador, along with José María de Heredia, the diplomat appointed by France in 1833, described the gored horses:

> I watched – like me, you laugh at the sight! –
> As, with desperate bounds
> Trailing a heavy mass of guts
> The disembowelled horses ran.[2]

Formerly a Spanish symbol, the bull was now a Mexican one, since it was being sourced from local ranches.

The traveller Isidore Loewenstern saw a Spanish-style *corrida*[3] attended by the re-elected president, Antonio López de Santa Anna (1853–5),

a former *practico* (amateur bullfighter): 'As far as I could see, the only difference was in the pusillanimity of the Mexican bulls, which are not as strong or fierce as the European ones. Often the bull is so terrified or so cowardly that the matador, the man who kills it, is unable to bring it against his sword.' Bulls that ran away were captured by lasso. Most Mexicans preferred cockfighting or the widespread *Charrería* featuring horse-riding gymnasts, which had become a national sport and a social pageant. The riders showed off their sumptuous trappings and remarkable physical abilities. The *carrera* (races) took place daily along avenues in the towns. In Venezuela, riders performed in the dangerous *coleados* (catching the bull by the tail); some 40 *distinguidos coleadores*, including General Juan Antonio Sotillo and various prominent figures, followed the bulls at a gallop, overtook them and caught them by the tail; then, turning back the way they had come, they toppled the bulls. The animals crashed to the ground suffering multiple fractures, as did the horsemen occasionally.[4] In Colombia in 1883 one traveller saw some Gineta-style (knees tucked up) showmen on horseback chasing a bull in an enclosed square (probably in Bogotá), but the main attraction was the sight of one hundred superb horses.[5]

Mexican bullfight poster.

All the travellers were struck by the remarkable craze for cockfighting, which was even more popular than bullfighting. These fights seem to have predated colonization.[6] The soldiers placing wagers wore round cages on their heads containing a precious *Jerezano* rooster, exported early to South America. Enormous sums were wagered, the results of which could instantly make people into slaves or wealthy landowners. Cockfights were banned as early as 1688, then by the Bourbons. Gallodromes (covered cockfighting spaces) appeared in the eighteenth century. As was the case with bullfighting, people claimed that the cocks' easy life was ample justification for torturing them. This voluntary tax enriched the coffers of an administration that nonetheless denounced its immorality. Retired matadors would breed cocks.

Fights organized between mismatched animals were very popular. At a one-off festival, 'the crowd flocked to the Plaza de los Toros to watch the fight between a Mexican bull and a Bengal tiger . . . An immense cage made of beams . . . measuring 20 to 22 metres' was set up in the bullring. The bull became the emblem of the Mexican nation while the tiger represented the French. The bull, with its shortened horns, seemed to be dying after one to two hours, but then the tables were turned. 'A shout went up, the crowed went wild . . . the *leperos* screamed, the social elite shouted themselves hoarse . . . the music struck up a triumphal march "*viva el toro, vivan los mexicanos, mueren los franceses*"'. The bull, which was presented to the government, died, but the French tiger recovered.

In Mexico in 1863 the largest Mexican political bullfight was held to celebrate the ceremonial entry of Maximilian, Emperor of Mexico, assisted by the armies of Napoleon III, who backed the South American supporters of slavery.[7] 'It was a bullfight for gentlemen toreadors held for their majesties . . . dressed in magnificent costumes . . . depending on the turns taken by the drama, the arena resounded constantly with opposing shouts of *bravo toro, fuera toro, a muerte el toro*, mingled with . . . the cheers of *viva el imperador*.

'Battle between a Lion and a Bull', illustration in *Le Petit Journal* (December 1894).

Alas, how many of those lips that repeatedly shouted those patriotic cheers, would one day utter the sinister cry of *Muera el Imperador*?' In actual fact, once Maximilian had been assassinated, silence reigned in the bullring. Benito Juarez, the 'Abraham Lincoln of Mexico City', banned bullfighting first in his native Oaxaca in 1861. Subsequently, after a bullfight that resulted in various deaths and a campaign by opponents,

the Mexican congress banned bullfighting in the federal district by article 87 of the Ley de Dotación de Fondos Municipales, which was passed on 28 November 1867.[8] The ban was lifted in 1887 after Porfirio Díaz had returned to power.

In France, a President of the Republic who had become Emperor with absolute power introduced bullfighting north of the Pyrenees. In 1850 in Europe bullfighting was still exclusively

Spanish, but everything changed with the coup of 2 December 1851 when Louis Bonaparte came to power. A government backed by a formidable police force and army, and which imprisoned or exiled any potential republican agitators, no longer had anything to fear from mass demonstrations, although it soon sought to win popular support by pandering to plebian tastes. In 1852 at Pont-Saint-Esprit (near Bayonne), Eugénie de Montijo watched a *Course Landaise* 'made more exciting with a few borrowings from the Spanish: although there were no picadors, the bull was killed'.[9] Due to pressure brought to bear by Spanish entrepreneurs, a Spanish *corrida* that had been rejected by the prefect was suddenly authorized, perhaps owing to the Empress's intervention. It was held in a temporary bullring at Pont-Saint-Esprit. There were several *corridas* held between 21 and 24 August 1853. The young Imperial couple were flaunting their power. This spectacle was reported in *L'Illustration*: in the 60 boxes of the temporary bullring 'Spanish women and . . . all the gilded society of the bathing season . . . [showed off] their dazzling wealth'. The exploits of Cúchares were also described with great admiration.

In 1854 the first practical French work in defence of bullfighting was published, illustrated by José Vallejo and written by Oduaga Zolarde (Aguado Lozar!), the Navarrian impresario of the famous matador Cúchares. The *Réveil des Landes* denounced a 'venture rivalling the *Courses Landaises*'.

Bullfighting pictures took Paris by storm at the Universal Exhibition of 1855. That same year, Cúchares (born 1818), who had emerged from the abattoirs of Seville as a young man, came up against El Chiclanero. They competed in the bullring, playing it for laughs, but when the ailing

Chiclanero died, Cúchares monopolized the Madrid bullring, with 322 appearances in 28 years. Cúchares was among the first to cross the Atlantic, but died of yellow fever in Havana in 1868. Double acts became popular: Lagartijo, nicknamed the Caliph (of Córdoba), killed 5,000 bulls in the course of his career. From 1868, in the arena, on paper and in cafés, he pitted himself against the sombre Frascuelo, who was often gored, but so skilled at killing that he was said to be 'made of bronze', and was the king of the Madrid bullring until 1890. He married a consummate technique with the characteristic ease of his effective, rhythmic sequence of passes. Each matador had a specific character, whether attractive or dull, cheerful or gloomy, sometimes even 'delicious', which was defined by the way he moved.[10] The appearance of bullfighting was changing. Technical manoeuvres were steadily acquiring grace and beauty, and accounts were becoming increasingly divorced from reality, causing people to forget what the bull was enduring.

THE BULLFIGHT AND ART

In France in the nineteenth century bullfighting became a more popular subject for engravers than for painters, while in Spain Delacroix sensed 'the quivering shadow of the great painter' Goya. In his *Journal* he wrote that art stopped where reality began. Art meant transcending nature. Delacroix's *Picador* was not drawn from nature, but copied from Carnicero. Numerous French painters visited Spain without painting many bullfights.

Countless bullfighting souvenirs were sold around Spanish bullrings. A documentary work about painters born around 1830, showed incidental aspects of the bullfight (Manuel Cabral y Aguado Bejarano, Manuel Castellano), the

Ignacio Zuloaga, *Women on the Balcony*, from *Le Figaro Illustré* (1903).

Nicaise de Keyser, '*Bravo Toro*', 1880–81, oil on canvas.

bullring, the accidents (José de Chavez), the *Tercios* (Roberto Domingo y Fallola) and, around 1880, rustic festivals (Nicolas Ruiz de Valdivia, Gustave Colin, Ignacio Zuloaga). In the early 20th century, among portraits of matadors (Daniel Vázquez Díaz), Ignacio Zuloaga (1870–1945), who was living in Paris, initiated Rilke into bullfighting, although not his friend, Rodin. His virtuoso technique was ideal for depicting society women flaunting themselves in the boxes at the bullring. Like fashionable Salomé, their impassive nonchalance when watching these bloody scenes aroused their admirers. The *género castizo* ('*espagnolades*') did not always impede talent, as could be seen by the work of José Elbo (1804–1846), but J. D. Bécquer lived in exile in Madrid and his son depicted the harrowing side of Seville.

After the scandal of the *Déjeuner sur l'herbe* (1863), Manet became interested in a photograph of the Madrid bullring, which he then drew on for his *Incident in a Bullfight*. This work was exhibited at the Salon of 1864, where it was ridiculed by a caricaturist, who transformed the distant bulls into snails. Manet cut up the painting in annoyance, but kept the magnificent fragments; the *Dead Toreador* fragment is now in the National Gallery of Art, Washington, DC.[11] His bold, foreshortened figure was inspired by a canvas attributed to Velázquez, an artist whom he had just discovered, so the painting was not a homage to a matador he had watched being killed. His letter to Astruc of 17 September 1865 described his emotion on seeing the horses 'gored by the bull's horns, the army of *chulos* trying to draw the furious beast away'. On his return, the *Matador Saluant* (1866) and *Victorine Meurent en costume d'espada* depicted the Spanish ballet on tour in Paris, where Spanish fashions had reached their peak. Manet painted four bullfighting scenes, including one showing the bull being killed. The true

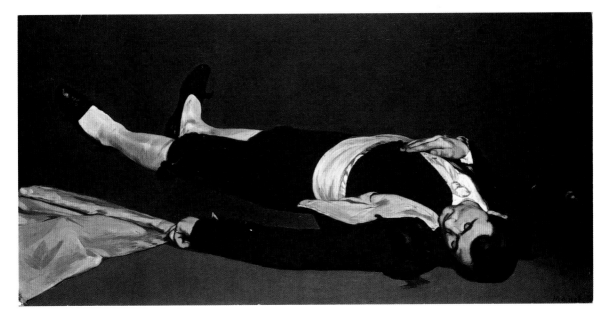

Edouard Manet, *The Dead Toreador*, 1864, oil on canvas.

Edouard Manet, *The Matador's Salute*, 1866–67, oil on canvas.

Edouard Manet, *Spanish Ballet*, 1852, oil on canvas.

Edouard Manet, *The Bullring in Madrid*, 1865, oil on canvas.

revelation of his trip was Velázquez, not the bullfight, which he described in just a few words in a letter to Baudelaire:[12] 'The brilliant, glittering and dramatic effect of the bullfight I saw.' Manet drew only one conclusion: 'It was worth the trip just for Velázquez.'[13] Several engravings depicted Spanish herds or Mariano Camprubi in the role of a *torero*; he also painted tambourines in aid of the flood victims of Murcia (1879).[14]

Lithography and other media led to a rapid rise in the popularity of travel sketches as single-sheet prints, as posters, and as book illustrations. In 1826 in France Baron Taylor brought out *Le Voyage pittoresque*, which was immediately translated into English and which described the military expedition to Spain of the Sons of St Louis. The French conquerors of Algeria crossed Spain at the same time as Montes achieved his first successes. *Le Tour du Monde*, then *Le Petit*

Journal, circulated illustrated accounts of bull-fighting. From 1864, the French benefited from new railways that made it easier to travel to the Spanish bullrings.

Around 1800 in Europe a generation of bull-fighting illustrators emerged,[15] such as Pharamond Blanchard (1805–1873), who collaborated with Madrazo on the album of royal festivals in Madrid in 1833, published by Goupil. Victor Adam, who specialized in lavish military subjects, published *Toro* (1830) in French and Spanish. The popular bilingual Éditions Turgis, which were even distributed in New York, printed portraits of *toreros*. The *Handbook for Travellers in Spain* (1834) by Richard Ford showed the Alcalá bull-ring in Madrid and the celebrations of sovereignty held on the Plaza Mayor for the Infanta, Isabella (1833). In 1843 the English linguist and anti-Catholic George Borrow published a bestseller of his travels on behalf of the Bible Society, *The Bible in Spain*. Last but not least, in 1844, an *España pintoresca y artistica*, followed by *Función de Toros* (1844) were brought out by Francisco de Paula van Halen.

Some strong artistic personalities appeared. The excellent German animal artist Wilhelm Gail (1804–1890), who had been in Spain since 1832, was supported by the Crown Prince Frederick William, to whom he dedicated his recollections, *Erinnerungen*. *The Spanish Bull Fights* (1850) by Lake Price described the social life in the bull-rings of Madrid, Seville and Cadiz. The draughts-manship of Juan José Martinez Espinosa was reminiscent of Jacques Callot in his treatment of the melee of horses and bulls. No pity or indignation is present in these works.

Around 1850 some international collective works came out, such as *L'España* by Manuel Cuendias, *Espagne Pittoresque, Artistique et*

Poster advertising a bullfight in Bayonne, 1897.

J. F. Lewis, *The Matador*, from *Sketches of Spain and Spanish Character* (1836).

Edouard Manet,
The Bullfight, c. 1866,
oil on canvas.

J. H. Clark, *General View of a Spanish Bullfight*, 1813.

Gustave Doré, 'The Entrance of the Picador', lithograph for
Charles Davillier's *Le Voyage en Espagne* (1860).

Monumentale (1848), *Spanien und die Spanier*,
and the anthologies of the *Semana Periodico
Universal* of Madrid or the *Anales del Toreo* by
José Velázquez y Sanchez (Seville, 1868). *L'España*
by the little-known Simons (Lemercier, 1880),
published illustrations by Alexander von Wagner.
These drawings, which were already expressionist
in style, denounced the terrible suffering inflicted
on the horses. For ten years (1862–72), Gustave
Doré illustrated the *Tour du Monde*. Doré accompanied Charles Davillier on the latter's tenth trip
to Spain in August 1861. The texts described a
cruelty that the images avoided: 'The bullfighting
public is indifferent to the sight of all this suffering
. . . as soon as a horse had fallen, the *muchachos*
came over and hit its nostrils with sticks to see

if it could still be used'.[16] The vehemence of the
draughtsmanship, underpinned by its spectacular
framing, passed for what was in fact a spurious
realism. This was an over-the-top, imposing bullfight: nothing was more vivid, nothing was more
bogus, and nothing was better able to give sub-
stance to the Romantic notion of the bullfight.

The black and white reproduction of the
illustrations removed all the blood from the
bullring, the weapons embedded in a living body
showed only their beribboned handles, and no
engraving would risk showing the horses' gaping
wounds in detail.

OPERA AND DANCE

It was around this time that the gypsy girl Carmen became the appointed ambassadress of a type of bullfight that was evoked rather than described. Published by Mérimée under financial pressure, this short novella of 1845, a recollection of conversations at the house of his Spanish friends, was transformed into an opera libretto in 1875, written by Meilhas and Halévy for Georges Bizet. Premiered in Paris by Célestine Galli-Marié in 1875, the performance was a flop from which Bizet did not survive. However, from 1884 onwards, the singer performed *Carmen* 1,200 times in Europe.[17] Carmen's character contravened the feminine stereotype imposed by society, being in charge of her own destiny to the bitter end. In the libretto, the matador's fight mimicked the battle of love. However, several directors distorted the opera by killing a bull in real life, which incensed Mexican fans in 1994: in the

Nadar's photograph of Célestine Galli-Marié in *Carmen* at the Opera Comique, Paris, in 1884.

Abanico de toreros ('fan' cape manoeuvre performed by the *toreros*), Madrid, photomontage.

arena, the violinists rebelled and the children in the chorus lamented the carnage wreaked by *torero* Jorge Gutierrez.[18]

Bizet's *Carmen* and Murger's *Vie de Bohême* (1852), as well as an edict by Charles III (1783) allowing gypsies into Spain, where they lived in Triana, made these colourful folk fashionable. The gypsies fired the popular imagination: they held bullfights in the evenings in the pasturelands. One performer, Rafael de Paula, a murderer, was said to have come out of prison to fight bulls. The gypsies embodied the anti-economy, the poetics of energy, the exceptional and the extreme.[19] In actual fact, very few matadors were gypsies and even fewer had been to prison: in 1878, out of 15,973 prisoners, there were only five bullfighters![20] A somewhat caricatured form of the *cante hondo* made its appearance in the taverns. Gypsy dance was characterized by the distance kept between partners, alternating attraction and repulsion, just as a repeated move towards the bull attempts to conceal technique. Sinking the chin towards the chest was a technique used in singing. The disdainful impassivity

Edouard Bertin (1875–1957), *Carmen, sketch for the stage set for Act IV, the entry of the circus into Seville.*

G. Marchetti, *A Musical Torero indicates the Site of the Future Universal Exhibition of 1889 where Bullfights will be held*, from an illustrated supplement to *Figaro* (1 December 1888).

Mariano Fortuny y Madrazo (1838–74), watercolour sketch of a bullfight with an injured picador.

of the dancers and their tantalizing bearing might have inspired *toreros* in search of a new style.

Traditional Spanish dance won admirers for its ethnological and technical curiosity value; Petipa studied Andalusian dance and staged a *Carmen* after Mérimée in 1845. Most of the Spanish bolero dance troupes in Europe between 1840 and 1870 staged *pas de deux*, *pas de trois* or groups danced by toreadors in costume (who were often women showing off their legs). Taglioni appeared in a *Gitana* (1838). Mariano Camprubi and Dolores Serral specialized in Spanish dance. The *Maja de Sevilla* (Paris, 1855, Porte Saint-Martin) or the *Perla de Madrid* (Paris, Odéon, 22 April 1867) became very popular. Much later, the aestheticization of bullfighting through dance occurred unexpectedly in Paris in 2005, when Henry-Jean Servat staged a production of *La Traviata*. The opera programmes stated that the reference to bullfighting was danced (II, 2) in order to denounce the 'abominable massacres' that took place in bullfighting.

By becoming a political issue, the violence of bullfighting was pressed into service by many dictatorial regimes in South America; and it was, of course, a usurper who established bullfighting in France. But more often than not, bullfights served as a pedestal for the men in power, who hijacked the spectators' fascination for cruelty to consolidate their position. The visual arts lent their support to the spread of bullfighting outside Spain, contributing heavily to the influx of bullfights in France. Furthermore, they attracted European tourists to the terraces.

Moving a herd of bulls in Morata de Taluña (Spain), *c.* 1895, photograph.

seven

Beyond Spain

By the late nineteenth century Spain had established itself as the leader in building new bullrings. Following Guadalajara (1861) and Zamora (1879), new rings were constructed in Salamanca, Toledo, Jerez, Madrid and Santander. Since the 1850s the railways had been providing transport for matadors and bulls (one poster pictured a bull that had escaped from its crate!), and from 1860 special trains were laid on for bullfights, making the bullring more of a tourist attraction.[1] The number of Spanish bullfight newspapers escalated from 40 in 1880 to over 100 in 1890. The middle classes, who organized popular leisure activities, held bullfights as part of their programmes. Though during the Spanish agricultural crisis prior to 1880, sales and prices of bulls suddenly increased, the age of fighting bulls dropped to four years old, saving breeders a year of pasturing.[2] Increasingly, bullfighting was becoming a national entertainment. One of the first novelists to tackle the subject was Mariano de Cavia, who published *De pitón a pitón* ('From horn to horn') in 1891. This was in the golden age of profitable, positive press coverage for bullfighting. The foundation of various societies for the protection of animals in Spain, albeit fairly late, bore witness to Spanish opposition. The animal protection society in Cadiz (1872) entreated the clergy to oppose the macho violence of the matador, which children first learned from toys, and which was denounced by writers like Raphael Alberti.[3] There were several fruitless attempts to introduce legal bans on bullfighting; in October 1882 the state gained control of the spectacle and institutionalized it. A penal code bill (19 December 1884) brought in by Francisco Silvela proposed taking disciplinary action against anyone who 'needlessly and cruelly maltreated animals in public' (Article 534) but it was thrown out.[4] In 1894 the Republicans vainly submitted the terms of an act to the Spanish government: 'Through its barbarity, this spectacle arouses the crudest instincts and, because of it, Spain is lagging behind the civilized nations that are trying to reduce violence. It is against the law.'[5]

In 1904 the Catholic Church requested that Sunday bullfights should hitherto be held on Mondays, which generated a political controversy. The socialist party continued to condemn the disastrous social consequences caused by the big ranches who hired low-paid workers, and the breeders demonstrated in Madrid, with the bullfighter Luis Mazzantini at their head, retorting that 360 hospital beds would be lost along with the bullfights. The newspaper *El Socialista* condemned the barbarity of this degrading spectacle and bullfighting entered Spanish political

Emile Bayard, cover of the December 1886 supplement to *Figaro Illustré*.

debate.[6] Eugenio Noel became one of the emblematic writers for opponents of bullfighting, but he also attacked flamenco. The fusion of these two ideas, bullfighting and flamenco dancing, was transferred into images, the guitar replacing the matador's sword (*Le Figaro illustré*). Eugenio Noel reused Jovellanos' economic argument. Along with Unamuno, he stressed the disastrous social repercussions and the harmful impact of extreme cruelty on spectators; he died in 1936, a prophet of the atrocities to come. He suggested replacing the 'seated sport' of the bullring with alternative sports activities, at a time when football was gaining popularity. He proposed that Spain should be regenerated through authentic cultural values. Colourful, impassioned and *vociferando*, he was targeted by bullfighting fans who condemned his so-called paranoia. It is even more ridiculous that Noel's unfortunate condemnation of flamenco is now assumed to negate his criticism of bullfighting.

THE SPANISH CORRIDA IN SOUTH AMERICA

Between 1887 and 1895, half a million Spaniards from the Atlantic coast, particularly Cadiz, settled in South America. However, some of the major Spanish-speaking countries passed progressive bans prohibiting bullfighting organizations to build bullrings, for example in Argentina in 1856. In Uruguay, bullfighting was banned in 1890. In Cuba in the 1890s the patriot José Marti denounced bullfighting as a reminder of the country's colonial past and slavery.[7] Baseball was regarded as a 'spectacle of lights compared with bullfighting, a barbarous spectacle'. Antonio Prieto organized a crusade against what he termed a 'shameful spectacle'. On 10 October 1899 the U.S. military government officially suppressed bullfighting. The activist Jeannette Ryder founded a society for the protection of children and animals in 1906. In 1898 a law in Costa Rica forbade killing the bull in the ring (renewed on 6 August 1968 and 20 September 1989). Last but not least, the bullfighting ban in Mexico by the decree of 7 October 1916 was the work of the most intrepid Mexican reformer, Venustiano Carranza (murdered in May 1920), who updated the ban passed in 1867 by Benito Juarez.[8]

Shortly before 1850, Lima, the true capital of bullfighting in Peru, which was now served by railways and steamboats, held performances by some 30 *toreros*, a number of whom were Spanish. A so-called Spanish style of bullfighting was performed both by Díaz Lavi, brother of the famous Manuel, said to be a Spanish gypsy, as well as by Angel Valdez (born 1838), who was the idol of Acho for half a century. One ranch, which imported bulls from the Duke of Veragua in Spain and from Miura, set up business at Pachacamac, in an Andean valley. It also incorporated a school, but was destroyed during the Pacific war (1879–83).[9] The recollections of Fuentes, a lawyer in Lima, as well as those of the Pradier-Fodéré family, who lived in Lima for twenty years,[10] and of several travellers attracted by the bullring's fame, raised doubts about the orthodox Spanish flavour of the spectacles. The mounted *capea* (free-for-all where amateurs are allowed to cape the bull), the practice of impaling the bull on a huge lance fixed in the ground, and the casual cruelty shown towards participants, particularly the Indians, were regular sights in this hotbed of heavy drinking, where the hefty consumption of strong spirits was commonplace.

> The *Mojarrero* never enters the arena till the bull appears to him no larger than a dog . . . 'It is too big yet; let us take another glass!' . . . if there are a few toreros half disembowelled, if the Indian *mojarreros* have been tossed up into the air; in short, if there have been plenty of injuries and bloodshed, the day is considered brilliant . . . the crowd will shout '*completa! soberbia (Excellent! Superb!)*)!'[11]

Camille Pradier-Fodéré described its unchanged picturesque appeal. The soldiers, the bull wearing *enjalmas*, tortured in the bullpen, even burned, the mounted *capea*, the *banderillas de fuego*, the riot of fireworks, the military parades, the exploits of the 'zambo-negroes',

the *capeadores* on their superb horses, the blood-thirsty instincts of the spectators and finally killing the bull the Spanish way: 'When all these emotions have been spiced with chicha, beer, brandy . . . you can, when the evening comes . . . congratulate yourself that the day has been well spent.' In 1850 the *aficionado* Radiguet described a bullfight held in honour of General Vivanco, who attended in person;[12] the *paseo* (initial parade) was distinctly Spanish, but variety acts (*mojigangas*) continued to be popular, although restricted by the law of 28 October 1892 that banned animal fighting.

In Venezuela, Caracas had three bullrings which were built before the 'generals' republic' was in place in 1867. Venezuela was undergoing modernization, with its metal aqueducts (1888) and the arena of the Gran Circo Metropolitano (1892) partly constructed of cast iron by the engineer Malusina, who had arrived from North America. After 1900 hydroelectric power made it possible to hold spectacles in the evenings. In 1863, the first suit of lights worn by matador Cuatrodedos, his *cuadrilla* and Antonio León's bullfighting school claimed to draw their inspiration from the Spanish technique.[13] Around 1900, a manual of Spanish bullfight vocabulary appeared, as did dedicated critics and correspondents from the Spanish press. The matador Frascuelo, who had been in Latin America since 1869, returned to Caracas around 1890, but the dissatisfied crowd rioted and burned down the bullring, coining the term *frascuelada*. It was inevitable that women should take up bullfighting, and one *torera* (Laura López) made a name for herself as 'the bull's sweetheart before she killed it'. The bullrings of Bogotá, Colombia (1890), La Paz, Bolivia (1888) and Quito, Ecuador (1905) competed with Caracas. In 1894 Eduardo Miura's bull, named Generoso, killed a picador and a horse. The Society for the Protection of Animals, which was extremely active, obtained a ban that same year (8 June) against killing bulls in the ring, similar to the Portuguese style of bullfighting, followed by a decree of 1897 that stated that 'the death of the *toro de lidia* is cruel and immoral'.[14]

In Mexico, the ban passed by Benito Juarez was abolished in 1887. Montes' treatise was re-published in Mexico City in 1887. The Spaniard Prieto Cuatrodedos joined forces with a banker to build an arena in Lower California (1899, destroyed in 1912) and bullfights were introduced there by Gonzales Rubio. Ponciano Díaz's style of bullfighting was more Mexican than Spanish, but he was very successful in Spain. During the nineteenth century Mexican ranches were supplying the rings with bulls, which were rarely crossed with Spanish breeds before 1900. Before the agrarian reform of 1910 there were about ten such ranches, many of which were in Tlaxcala (a region of Mexico City). Two ranches in particular, Laguna and Piedras Negras (founded in 1890), which did use Spanish cattle, were renowned for providing very aggressive bulls from 1900 onwards.[15]

Only around fifteen of the 600 identifiable Mexican *toreros*, documented until 1958,[16] were born in the 1880s, like Freg and Gaona. There were more *toreros* of the same generation as Arruza, born between 1920 and 1930. Most of the *toreros* came from a district of Mexico City and later from the regions of Guadalajara and Leon de las Aldamas, like Gaona or Aguascalientes. The most famous *torero*, Rodolfo Gaona (1888–1975), made his debut in Mexico City in 1905, and was a bullfighter for about 20 years. He competed against renowned Spanish bullfighters like Joselito.[17]

Luis Mazzantini (1856–1926), who was born Basque but was of Italian descent, trained in a bullfighting school rather than in the ring. His so-called effective *estocada* was very theatrical. He fought bulls in Montevideo from 1881, before taking his *alternativa* (a ceremony during which the novice bullfighter is presented to the crowd as a fully-fledged matador) in Seville. He performed in Cuba in 1886 and negotiated an exorbitant contract there (30,000 gold *pesos* for fourteen bullfights). Latin American fees at that time were twice as high as Spanish payments. Faced with dwindling success in Spain, the Spanish matador Antonio Fuentes (1869–1938) went to South America to finish his career. Mazzantini appeared at the Universal Exhibition in Paris in 1889 and toured South America, where his affair with Sarah Bernhardt was the talk of the town.[18] Porfirio Díaz, president of Mexico in 1877–80, was returned to power for the long period of 1884–1911, during which he re-established *corridas* as part of Mexico's culture.

The celebrated Mexican matador Rodolfo Gaona became one of the principal Mexican ambassadors in Spain. He was one of the first to take the *alternativa* in Madrid (in 1908), his three compatriots making do with taking their *alternativa* in Barcelona or Badajoz. Fifty-six per cent of Mexican matadors took their *alternativa* in Spain, particularly in Madrid, Luis Freg in 1911, but some repeated their *alternativa* four times over! Peruvians followed suit: they were often well received in Barcelona or Benidorm.[19] The practice was stopped by Spanish bans and World War Two.

THE SPANISH *CORRIDA* VERSUS THE *LOI GRAMMONT*

Bullfighting was introduced by force in France in 1853, soon after the law known as the Loi Grammont of 2 July 1850, which punished cruelty towards animals following the example of Martin's Act of 1822 in Britain. As was the case with slavery, animal protection came up against some powerful economic interests, driven mainly by the importance of animal traction.[20] Grammont's first bill, which proposed to penalize any act of animal cruelty, was crushed by what was tantamount to a political conspiracy. On 2 July 1850 a deputy spoke out against it: 'I only want . . . to suppress those acts which, through their seriousness and public nature, undermine public morality . . . you will be amply protecting animals without striking a blow at ownership, which consists in using and abusing.' Grammont replied: 'You are completely destroying the structure of the law.'[21] As a result, quarries, mines, slaughterhouses and knackers'

yards remained bastions of maltreatment, and the enclosed bullrings with their so-called 'wild' bulls, were safe from the law.

However, the Loi Grammont was so innovative that it was supported by opponents of bullfighting, who had recently gathered together in Societies for the Protection of Animals (SPA). Victor Schœlcher and Doctor Henri Blatin, heroes of the anti-slavery vote in France, were backed by liberal moralists who were 'naturally hostile' to bullfighting: it was felt that the Republic should preserve the moral code of the Enlightenment, but proponents insisted that an equal fight glorified man.[22] *Aficionado* historiographers have put forward the argument that Mediterranean peoples have an innate passion for bullfighting. However, this claim is not borne out by the facts. The *aficionado* Auguste Lafront acknowledged that the introduction of bullfighting in France initiated 'forty years of uncertainty'. It was not that there were more Spanish *corridas* held in the South of France than in other areas of

Bullfight, Arles, c. 1913; written on the back of the postcard is 'We are getting ready to go to the bullfight today'.

102   ARLES. — Les Arènes. — Combat de Taureaux. — LL.

The day of a kill in the bullring, Nîmes, postcard, *c.* 1910.

France after 1854, but that they were more famil-iar. Supporters of the old-style provincial bull events, formalized during the Revolution, were opposed to the Spanish spectacles. Arles, capital of the *Course Camarguaise* (a traditional sport in which rosettes are snatched from the horns of young cattle), resisted the Spanish-style *corrida* until 1892, some 30 years after Nîmes (1863), then banned it around 1900, and then again between 1923 and 1932. In the interim, just one bullfight was held each year.

The suppression of bullfighting led to popular unrest in 1884, which quietened once the ban was removed for the *Course à la Cocarde* (another name for the *Course Camarguaise*). Three Deputies from the South of France condemned Spanish bullfighting at the National Assembly. In 1900 the Gironde region denied that there was any link between the two spectacles. Bull-fighting achieved limited success in its reputed strongholds of Bayonne and Mérignac. One postcard showed a matador dealing the death

blow before virtually empty terraces. The size of the audience decreased from the second perform-ance, as in Nîmes (1863). The mixed bullfights of Saint-Sever (1861), the absence of bullfighting in Dax until 1878, the lease cancelled in Bayonne in 1861 and 1862, showed either a lack of interest, or opposition to a style of bullfighting that was still called 'Spanish'.

The event was a complete failure in many French towns: the impresario Pablo Mesa failed in Périgueux, Agen and Poitiers (1866) and in The Hague (1868). The intense propaganda of the years between 1890 and 1910 reached the Atlantic coast (Rochefort-sur-Mer, 1897; Nantes, 1906; Saint Malo, 1912), and the southeast (Vichy, 1892; Lyon, 1894, for the Universal Exhibition; Roubaix, 1899; Reims, 1900; Autun, 1913). Occasional bullfights were held in Paris, Royan and Quimper in 1934, and in Limoges in 1935, among other places.[23] However, following the law of 5 April 1884, mayors were elected and, as a result, were able to oppose the prefects, who were representatives of central power. Paradoxically, the southerners adopted the Spanish bullfight as the spearhead of the French south: according to their simplistic philosophy, anyone who was opposed to bullfighting was deemed to be a northerner, and a Parisian, and therefore hostile to Mediterranean French people. Conversely, any *aficionado* was thought to support sound southern virtues. There were many Spanish expatriates in the south, and they supported the Spanish impresarios who had taken the French market by storm. The government did not cave in. Waldeck-Rousseau, Minister of the Interior, supported the Loi Grammont. Local bull events like the *Course Camarguaise* and the *Course Landaise* were accepted as sports federations,

while bullfights were regarded as spectacles (27 June 1884). An unexpected later account (1933) was provided by Henri de Montherlant, who observed that a tradition of bullfighting was not intrinsic to the South of France: the 'bullfights held in Bordeaux, Dax, the Eastern Pyrenees, the Alpes-Maritimes, etc. . . . are a spectacle that is not firmly established' and one that most spectators know nothing about. 'Why does the public enjoy these bullfights? Mainly because they can watch animals being maltreated'.[24]

THE INVENTION OF SPANISH LANGUEDOC

The World Fairs in America and France were intended as international showcases, exhibiting human types, folk spectacles and so-called

The bullring at Béziers showing the empty terraces, c. 1900.

ethnological objects. The St Louis World Fair in 1904 staged a bullfight as though it was from the Wild West, but it was declared unlawful by the indignant crowd, who burned down the amphitheatre.[25] Back in 1889 the Paris Exhibition lavishly celebrated the centenary of the French Revolution. Mazzantini was a friend of José Oller, who owned the Paris Olympia and the Moulin-Rouge, and organized shows at the Nouveau-Cirque. Mazzantini performed in the luxurious, electrified auditorium, which was often empty, on Rue Pergolèse, where bulls from the ranches of the famous Duke of Veragua were brought in, then killed out of sight of the spectators. The painter Gustave Popelin, son of the famous enameller and father of the future *aficionado* Claude Popelin, and Auguste Clarétie, director of the Comédie-Française, introduced the phrase *duel entre l'esprit et la matière* (the battle of mind over matter).[26]

Around the time of the International Exhibition of 1889, Buffalo Bill's Wild West Show organized by William F. Cody toured Southern France twice (1889 and 1905). It staged a fictional, romantic version of Manifest Destiny in the USA, showing 'how the West was won', although this process involved mass persecution of Native Americans, who participated in the Wild West Show wearing feathered costumes. In the wake of French regionalism, which set itself in opposition to the Parisian power base, various 'imagined communities' emerged, such as the Camargue, which became particularly famous due to the efforts of Baron Folco de Baroncelli-Javon, who had retired to his inhospitable lands between two branches of the Rhône.[27] Together with various scholars, among them Joseph d'Arbaud and the writer Frédéric Mistral, Baroncelli undertook to create an identity for the Camargue, which back then was inhabited mostly by mosquitoes. These

'Pawnee Bill's historic Wild West' poster, 1890s.

men adopted the authentic if not unique 'bull culture' as a symbolic marker of the Languedoc region and founded Félibrige, a literary and cultural society.

The Buffalo Bill Show acted as a catalyst on the naive Baroncelli; the Occitan people of Southern France were thought to have been the victims of a genocide, like the Native Americans, who they claimed as their brothers. Baroncelli corresponded for twenty years with Jacob White Eyes, an Oglala Sioux, had himself photographed in his plumed costume and created a 'purebred Camargue man', drawing his inspiration both from Mistral and the Wild West. He invented

'The Indomitable Bull', an illustration from *Le journal Illustré* (April 1864).

'a folkloric haute couture' for the Camargue *gardians* or herdsmen, a cross between gauchos and cowboys, and he came up with the now cult of the famous *levée des tridents* (brandishing of the tridents) of 1921. His *gardians* performed at the Marseille Colonial Exposition in 1931.

The influence exerted by Baroncelli and Charles Maurras on Mistral hastened the adoption of bullfighting by the South of France, particularly as a result of Mistral's about-face. On a memorable occasion in 1894, in the bullring at Nîmes, Mistral spoke out in praise of the bullfight (Spanish-style!): 'There's nothing here to justify the word barbarity. We cannot enjoy our bullrings by putting on cockfights or ordinary pigeon shoots in them.'

Politics entered the bullring in Nîmes with the bullfight of 16 September 1894, which was held against prefectural advice and therefore seen as symbolic of a southern victory over the north. The famous toreador Guerrita fought some highly belligerent bulls from Camara with remarkable flair. Two short-lived bullfight newspapers had been founded in Nîmes, *Le Toreo Franco-Espagnol* (1894–6) and the earlier and more influential review *La Mise à mort* (1892–6); both made the most of Guerrita's presence. The same year, the first bull killings took place in the ring at Arles. Guerrita took part in over 30 bullfights in France. The strength of the Duke of Veragua's bulls as well as the *toreros'* exploits made headline news in a press that was already tabloid in spirit. The dismissal of the Mayor of Dax for putting on unlawful bullfights provoked a discussion in the Chamber of Deputies and a consolidation of local council authority, but a Deputy from the Landes

A bullfight underway in the spectacular Roman amphitheatre at Nîmes.

region responded to a ministerial circular by advising prefects to ban Spanish bullfights. The symbolic police escort taking Mazzantini back to the border in 1895 made the headlines of *Le Petit Journal*, which portrayed the hero in his suit of lights to make the front page more eye-catching. Panache was in vogue. The burgeoning advertising industry adopted bullfighting. Campaigns like *Caramba heureusement Urgo est là* ('Caramba! Fortunately, Urgo is here' – Urgo was

Mazzantini being expelled from France into Spain, from *Le Petit Journal* (September 1895).

The Osborne winery in Andalucia used bulls and bullfighting themes in adverts.

then a major French company specializing in wound healing) or the *Voyage de la famille Bigorno en Espagne* (1910) did more for the spread of bullfighting than Gaston Doumergue, who, once he became President of the Republic, played down his *afición*. 'Bon points' (illustrated cards given to pupils to reward good marks), pictures that came with chocolate bars, and calendars in the *Figaro Illustré* accustomed people to images of bullfights that may have looked harmless in the illustrations but were anything but in the ring. These images trivialized bullfighting, and many politicians thought the subject unworthy of discussion.

The 'Affaire des Courses de Taureaux', judged on appeal in Limoges in 1898, provided bullfighting with an unexpected forum. An impassioned speech for the defence by Maître Roux defended these southern 'virile games', which he contrasted with the 'obscene blandness of Parisian cafés', an argument popularized by Edgar Quinet. He argued that the Loi Grammont, which was devoted to domestic animals, should not be applied to the

Toreador and bull on the Vulcan Safety Match matchbox.

A. Chalon, *Le Figaro Illustré* calendar for 1898.

bull, since it was a wild animal, although this was obviously not the case. By presenting the bull as prey, bullfighting became associated with hunting and by extension with the aristocracy and the judicial authorities, for whom it formed a characteristic marker of social superiority.[28]

By the end of the nineteenth century bullfighting in France did not appear to be so successful, despite specialist publications like the *Torero* (1890–1944). There were various incidents in temporary bullrings, for example in Deuil (a region of Paris), where the bull leaped onto the public terracing. Private bullfights, organized by the wealthy sugar manufacturer Lebaudy, unleashed the fury of the press and attracted the attention of the journalist Séverine, who had defended striking women at Lebaudy's sugar refineries. *Le Figaro illustré* caricatured the sugar producer. In 1901, in Nîmes, bullfighting was 'a financial disaster . . . which no one could have foreseen'. The impresario, on the brink of bankruptcy, declared it was impossible to interest people in this spectacle. The town council founded a bullfighting club and hired the cheapest bullring, but to no avail. In 1902, the cheap seats accounted for 75.6 per cent of admissions; soldiers were given virtually free seats (5.9 per cent). The number of subscribers dropped (299 in 1909; 207 in 1910). In 1909 an appeal was made to the bullring in Madrid. In 1911, during the last days of the Socialist Party Congress, the arena was at last packed with congress participants. In 1912 subscriptions numbered 326, with 850 free tickets and 7,092 unsold, but showing an increase of 55 per cent over 1901. Ticket sales for the arena represented 56.6 per cent of filled seats, with the expensive seats accounting for 8.8 per cent. The takings improved, so the *droit des pauvres* (a tax on the revenue from spectacles) could be paid.

In 1912, taking account of the soldiers, regional *aficionados*, subscribers and free seats, the bullring welcomed 11,226 people.[29]

Three major political debates marked the development of the legal position of bullfighting. The Bertrand bill of 1900 is the best documented. Waldeck-Rousseau, defender of the Loi Grammont in 1884, appeared to lose momentum; Gaston Doumergue's phrase became legendary: 'you realise how few friends men have, when animals have so many.' Doumergue introduced the idea of authorizing bullfights, but only in towns where this spectacle had existed permanently before 1900. A bill aimed at banning all animal fighting (this included the bull-against-horse attacks in the ring), was passed with 414 for and 67 against. Deputies from the north of France defended cockfighting; three Parisians and only 53 per cent of southern Deputies were in favour of a law which, in fact, never proceeded to the vote, so was not promulgated.[30] The brilliant conclusion drawn from this political episode by Octave Mirbeau was that 'A clear majority of citizens simply cannot ensure that a law is enforced . . . it is through such acts of cowardice, even less mysterious because they are electoral, that power has laid down its arms in the face of barbarity.'[31]

RENEWED OPPOSITION

The opposition of Caroline Rémy (alias Séverine, 1855–1929) to animal suffering of any kind was a key phase in feminism. A follower of Jules Vallès, she was with Émile Zola on the side of the miners of Decazeville, with the women on strike at Lebaudy's sugar refineries, and the women who died in the fire at the Bazar de la Charité. A militant feminist, joint founder of *La Fronde*, this beautiful woman posed for Louis

Pierre-Auguste Renoir, *Caroline Rémy ('Séverine')*, c. 1885,
oil on canvas.

Welden Hawkins (Musée d'Orsay) and Renoir.
Ridiculed by fans of bullfighting, her defence
of animals was glossed over by her biographers
until the twenty-first century.[32]

The attacks generated by bullfighting greatly
increased anti-feminist hatred. Caldine used the
age-old argument that Séverine was boosting
her declining fame by engaging in opportunist
political activities. The standard usurpative stereo-
types appeared; Séverine was endeavouring to
'make (her) style more masculine'. In Spain, someone wrote that women 'desecrate the virile nature
of bullfighting'. A German guide contained the
sentence: 'Wealthy ladies who protect animals
maltreat their maids and ignore the thousands
who are starving to death.' Henri de Rochefort

in *L'Intransigeant* (21 October 1904) wrote his
famous dictum: 'women are cows at least as much
as men are bulls.' Terms such as *hysterical, petites-
bourgeoises* and *sentimental* were used for women,
while men who were against both bullfighting and
the death penalty were insultingly called effemi-
nate and dubbed ridiculous sentimentalists.

Under the police regime of the Second Empire
(1863), Claude-Augustin Plantier, Bishop of
Nîmes, compromised himself by opposing bullfighting (politics played a key role in the appoint-
ment of bishops). He insisted that every Christian
'should refrain not only from torturing, but even
from offending, or worrying, any being in order
to divert himself from his sorrows'. He spoke out
against the dubious argument of the bullfight's
charitable function, saying that 'Purses which are
always empty for charity are easily untied for the
bullfights'. He also countered the exceptions made
for the South, whose latent racism he detected
with the apt sentence: 'People demand exceptions
to be made for the patch of land we inhabit as if,
because we live in Provence and the Languedoc,
we do not belong to the human race.' In 1885
his successor, Xavier-Louis Besson, commented
on the still valid Bull of Pius v of 1567 as well as
the reality of bullfighting: '(The bulls) offered up
gaping wounds, they breathed . . . their last groans
in front of 20,000 spectators . . . Nothing noble,
nothing grand, nothing useful . . . these bullrings (are) dishonoured by a pleasure which is a
disgrace.' A Catholic author, Frédéric Ozanam,
beatified in 1997, described a bullfight he had seen
in Biarritz to his brother before 17 September
1852 and worked on an article that was published after his death (15 September 1853) in
Le Correspondant:[33] 'My only distress was to
watch the poor animals tormented in such a barbaric manner and when the first one was killed,

An events programme, Seville, 1967.

we left with the same feeling that we would have carried away from the abattoir, if we had gone there for pleasure.[34] When Zola defended Captain Dreyfus, unjustly accused of treason, he wrote to Séverine to say that 'I am absolutely against bullfights, which are appalling spectacles whose senseless cruelty provides the masses with an education in blood and mud. The result will be a fine France indeed, on the eve of the twentieth century, if all the decent people don't stand in its way.'[35]

Like many opponents to the death penalty, Victor Hugo was a spokesman for suffering animals. He was against bullfighting on two counts, since it was both a public execution and an example of suffering exploited for a public entertainment. In *Les Derniers Jours d'un condamné*, he expressed indignation that executions could be made into a form of entertainment and described the spectators' horrible attentiveness. He denounced the hardheartedness of the religious man towards the suffering animal: the exhausted donkey saved a toad that was crushed by a priest in the rudest health. He came to a radical conclusion: 'We have tyrants, because we are tyrants.' He was president of an anti-vivisectionist association, but when bullfighting arrived in France with 'Napoléon-le-Petit', Hugo, a fervent admirer of many things Spanish, was in exile. Bullfighting spread when he was very old. Years previously, the animal protectors had published a phrase about bullfighting that may have been penned by Hugo: 'torturing a bull is like torturing one's conscience'. As Gandhi was to do, the writer took man's behaviour towards animals as a criterion of humanity.

Henri Achille Zo, *L'Ovation*, 1894, oil on canvas.

eight

The Influence of Art, Film and History

A painting by Bernardo Ferrandiz y Badenes, *¡Caballos, Caballos!* (*Horses! Horses!*) of 1877 depicted a nobleman gazing at his empty stables in despair after the bullfights; the *Ovation* (*c.* 1894) by Henri Achille Zo recorded the incredible enthusiasm provoked by the goring of the horses, the main loss leader of the spectacle. *España negra*, written in the 1880s by Verhaeren and illustrated by Dario de Regoyos, included images of tortured horses in the bullring. In Adolphe Gumery's painting *Les Coulisses de la corrida* (*c.* 1912), the prophetic expression of a horse dying in the midst of other disembowelled animals seems to be calling down a curse on the world. José Gutierrez Solana, who bore witness to the squalid side of Madrid, described these martyred horses. Elsewhere, socialists from Bilbao and Corunna were demanding a ban on bullfights in the name of agrarian reform.

After World War One there were fewer unwanted horses, and in 1928, a Spanish decree ordered that horses used in bullfights should be protected by a caparison. The killing of the bull thus became the main attraction in the ring, although the horses still suffered: terrorized, blindfolded, they were injured by the charging bulls, treated roughly by the riders, overburdened and often drugged. The organizers provided numerous spare mounts, clear proof of the injuries inflicted, despite the fact that bullfighters had begun to demand weaker, and therefore younger, bulls, which of course benefited the breeders.

THE ARTS

Bullfighting was now a popular subject for painting and literature. Various renowned writers strayed so far from reality as to abandon it entirely, creating a completely different, imaginary, spectacle. In *Sang et Lumières*, Joseph Peyré caricatured this new style of literary *torero* influenced by matador-writer Ignacio Sanchez Mejias (1891–1934). Surrealism preferred the subtle mutual image of praying mantises devouring each other to wholesale slaughter; it gave a fashionable cachet to any kind of 'theatre of cruelty' (after the drama of Antonin Artaud). Salvador Dalí developed hallucinogenic bullfights; he associated the image of the bull's horns with his moustaches. In Figueras, poles topped with horns-moustaches are the remnants of an epic bullfight of 12 August 1961. His encyclopaedic *Hallucinogenic Toreador* (1970) brought together his fetishist images, interspersed with flies and *toreros*.

The number of specialist magazines increased in Spain. *Sol y sombra*, *Ruedo* and *Digame* hired professional commentators, *revisteros*, who became popular, from Gregorio Corrochano

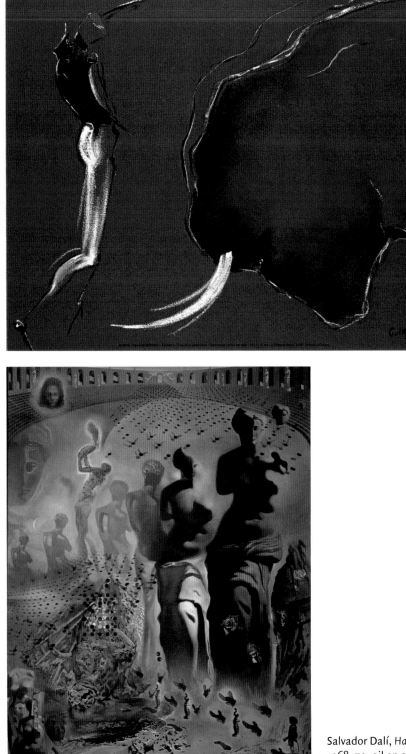

Pascal Guérineau, *Corrida II*, a recent art print.

Salvador Dalí, *Hallucinogenic Toreador*, 1968–70, oil on canvas.

Poster for the Plaza de Toros, Barcelona, 1912.

A 1928 poster for the Nueva Plaza de Toros, San Sebastian.

Ortega (1882–1961) to R. Capdevila, who covered Franco's 'victory bullfight' in the pro-Franco newspaper *ABC*. In France, some twenty bullfight magazines were founded between 1922 and 1933, including the *Toril* in Toulouse (1922–40) financed by the dictatorial Alfred Degeilh. Degeilh, who trained the likes of Auguste Lafront and Jean-Pierre Darracq, was harshly criticized by former

contributors for his portliness and his bullfighting tastes. Antonio Diaz-Canabate (1898–1980), one of Franco's war correspondents, frequently kept company with the poet Blaise Cendrars in France.

An incredible amount of skill went into the creation of bullfighting posters, which became genuine works of art. There are 1,567 posters in the archives in Valencia dating from 1832 to

1992, and Saragossa organized annual competitions, both for posters in giant format (100 x 240 cm), or miniaturized for flyers (11 x 32 cm) or for admission tickets. Specialist printers sold illustrations ready to be completed with the relevant information.[1] Photography was not highly valued. Animal painters specialized in the field of bullfight posters, particularly around Bilbao, famous for an *afición* who claimed to love the animals they condemned to painful deaths. The long vertical posters always showed a *muleta* pass: a matador with his back arched backwards, disproportionately elongated, dominating a black bull that appeared to be coiling around him. At the end of the century these posters began featuring various anecdotal details: an escaped bull attacking a milk donkey (1895), a locomotive speeding straight for the bullring (1917, Murcia), a music contest, a battle of flowers, some impressive cars (1930, Bilbao), folkloric costumes (1912, Valencia), everything except the reality of a bullfight, reduced to a few tame insets.

Films played a vital role in this euphemization. Representatives sent by the Lumière Brothers were entertained in Mexico by Porfirio Díaz. The jerky images of these early films, taken from a distance, showed crowds of participants moving about in the bullring. Mazzantini could be seen performing (1895); Edison filmed Mexican bullrings; Gaumont in 1909 shot the bullfighter Bombita; and Louis Feuillade photographed Machaquito in Nîmes. The film *Fiancés de Séville* (1915) sanctioned a sentimental view of bullfighting, since it contained bloodshed, a *femme fatale* and a virile matador presented in a flattering light. In 1916 *Sangre y arena* by Blasco Ibanez anticipated the 1922 silent version, *Blood and Sand*, which exploited the star status of Rudolf Valentino, followed by Rita Hayworth in the

1941 remake. Real *toreros* played themselves, like Marcial Lalanda in *Viva Madrid* (1928). The remakes of *Carmen* (one by Cecil B. DeMille in *c.* 1915) exploited the romantic myth and its sanitized bullring. The only fresh approach was the Walt Disney cartoon about the poetically pacifist bull, Fernando, who preferred flowers to fighting. The screenplay, based on a story by Munro Leaf, enjoyed the dual honour of pleasing Gandhi and annoying Hitler, who had it burned. The role played by Hollywood was enhanced in 1943 as a result of Roosevelt's political desire to humour Mexico and unite the nations. The aim of the Office for the Coordination of Inter-American Affairs was to amuse and entertain. Comedy bullfighting films, such as *What's the Matador?* (1942), featuring gags later reused by Laurel and Hardy (1945), were further additions to the tradition of comic bullfights.[2]

The Ballets Russes commissioned Picasso to design a matador costume for *Le Tricorne* (1919), followed by *En España* by Leo Staat, then *Ole Toro* by Michel Fokine. Nijinsky was never a fan of bullfighting, unlike Diaghilev, who said that 'a bullfight is a magnificent art. I know

A still from Rouben Mamoulian's 1941 film *Blood and Sand*.

A poster for the 1942 Mexican film *Seda, Sangre y Sol* ('Silk, Sunshine and Blood').

Pablo Picasso, Stage curtain for *Le Tricore*, premiered by the Ballets Russes in London, July 1919.

that they . . . will say that I am mad . . . Diaghilev always used that trick . . . I understand him and therefore challenge him to a bullfight – I am the bull, a wounded bull. I am God in the bull.'³ Various gypsy operas, such as Raoul Laparra's *Habanera*, did not show any bulls, but conjured up the world of bullfighting.

Eisenstein's drawings of 1932–3 were among the first to illustrate the intense erotic pleasure afforded by victims of torture, including animals.⁴ These numerous, hand-drawn images forcefully tackled anti-clerical caricature and religious

eroticism, denouncing ambiguous Catholic beliefs, women's virginity and their ecstasy before St Sebastian. Every wound inflicted on the bull represented an enjoyable act of sodomy that brought the ecstatic traveller to orgasm. The victim, the crucified bull, remained an outsider to the traveller's sexual delight, as in the Nordic paintings of *Christ Mocked*, in which the torturers link sexual pleasure and torture by means of obscene expressions and gestures.

Eisenstein's film *¡Que viva Mexico!* was halted in January 1932, when most of the Fiesta

Sergei Eisenstein, from a series of erotic-pornographic drawings, *La Matildona*, picking up a film project from 1931.

had not been filmed.[5] This bullfight (in its present state) abounds in comfortable, conventional, romantically unchallenging clichés: the *torero*, a good son full of respect for a selfless mother who accepts his uncontrollable passion, the spurious sacred-seeming presentation of a star confronting his destiny, the anxiety of the women on the terraces. Such platitudes seem out of kilter with such an innovative talent.

THE MYTHS OF HISTORY

Scholarly research undertaken on the Greek and Roman 'bull games' (by Beurier, 1897), and on the myths and rites centred on the bull in the Mediterranean (A. Alvarez de Miranda), as well as a fine archaeological exhibition in 1914 with some superb bronze heads of bulls and the dis-

covery of the rock paintings at Altamira in 1906 combined to make the archaic animal fashionable. By means of a simple metonymy (shifting the bull's ancientness onto the practice of bullfighting), people claimed that bullfighting was as old as time. In a civilization thought to be exhausted, a return to archaism seemed like a regenerative course of action. By lucky coincidence, the physical appearance of the matador Manolete (1917–47) was in keeping with this archaistic turn: 'Spindly, a gaunt face with a feverish expression . . . His style . . . almost hieratic . . . the way he fought bulls created an almost mystic feeling of expectation . . . a remarkable myth.'[6]

In 1894 Maurice Barrès celebrated the 'intoxicating force that rises up from carnage . . . it is a rejuvenating experience for humanity,' in his work *Du sang, de la volupté et de la mort*. Henri de Montherlant, obsessed with death on his return from war, believed he had found a 'rule of life' in an archaic style of bullfight. In Andalucia, welcomed by Belmonte and others, he wrote *Les Bestiaires*,[7] a book whose importance was anticipated by an intelligent article published (29 April 1926) in the *Toril*. *Les Bestiaires* provided bull-fighting fans with everything they needed: a specific technical approach to bullfighting, a pseudo sacrificial interpretation, a complete indictment of animal protection, described as the *terreur rose* (pink terror)! The hero, Alban, an archetype skilled in male chauvinist violence, advocated murder that was 'beneficial' and 'really creative' and expressed his sadism: 'What a priceless jewel this bull was! What a wonder! And what wouldn't he give to kill it.'

Like Mistral and Baroncelli-Javon, Montherlant was inspired by Cumont in the 1890s and then by Alfred Loisy, a professor at the Collège de France. He believed that the Mithraic cult included sacrifices of bulls, which was not actually the case: many of its worshippers, some of whom were vegetarians, mundanely ate chickens bought in the market at the foot of the illuminated image of Mithra, which represented the god in the process of slitting the throat of a bull. Montherlant sought to find enduring traces of Mithraism in Christianity, in order to regenerate the latter, which he felt was moribund. The writer turned his back on bullfighting in 1933: 'the brutal impact, the blood, the death, and the shock they produce are nonetheless – ah yes! let's come clean! – are nonetheless one of the ingredients of their pleasure . . . we must not let this boorish behaviour and this brutality take root where they are unforgivable.'[8]

LEIRIS

Although he did not much care for Montherlant, Leiris, in his autobiographical texts, shared the older man's fascination with death as well as his severe suicidal tendencies, having made several attempts to take his own life. He was fascinated by the pleasurable aspect of any violent death. Like many suicidal writers, he wrote 'for want

Adolphe Gumery, *Inner yard in the Plaza, c.* 1912, a postcard reproduction of the painting first seen at a Paris salon.

of living'.[9] This is why he believed 'literature . . . to be like bullfighting'. He highlighted the obvious eroticism of bullfighting: 'there is no need to appeal to the facts, or melt them in the crucible of symbolic interpretation to observe that bull-fighting is thoroughly immersed in an erotic atmosphere'.

His friend the painter André Masson was deeply affected by the bloodthirsty eroticism of animal torture, as expressed in *Le Jet de sang*. Traumatised by the war of 1914–18, the artist transposed his turmoil onto animals. For example,

after visiting an abattoir, he did not depict man's brutality towards animals, but a fight between animals, as if to justify the wickedness of the former by the brutality of the latter. He avoided any direct representation of bullfighting. His obsessive engravings for the *Miroir de la Tauro-machie* abounded in clefts, pelts, vaginas and phallic horns. Several matadors dared to admit openly that they experienced intense sexual pleasure: Pepe Luis Vásquez declared: 'I got a real thrill out of it, an incredible thrill out of it.' The matador Juan Posada detected the spectators'

André Masson, *The Spurt of Blood*, 1936, oil on canvas.

perverse enjoyment: 'People have a morbid desire to see what's going to happen today [15 April 2001] when faced with some aggressive *toros*.'[10] The character of Simone in Georges Bataille's *Histoire de l'oeil* (1928) 'was on tenterhooks from start to finish at the bullfight, in terror (which of course mainly expressed a violent desire) at the thought of seeing the toreador hurled up'.[11]

Leiris attended around 40 bullfights, mainly in Nîmes, in the circle of André Castel, an *aficionado* and wine expert. Several bullfighting poems by Leiris, the *Miroir de la Tauromachie* (1937–8) and the *Poèmes de Tauromachie* (1937) were written later than Bataille's *Histoire de l'oeil*. Myth was a popular topical subject at the Collège de Sociologie, where Leiris gave a lecture on 'Le Sacré dans la vie quotidienne'. He wrote the *Miroir de la tauromachie* as a poet,[12] but he composed this lecture as a renowned ethnologist, commenting that it was 'legitimized by the ethnographic pretext'.[13] Leiris supported his thesis on bullfighting with some poetically disparate ideas. The suit of lights became a 'sacerdotal costume' (p. 34). It was the bull's blood that was noble, while that of the disembowelled horses (which had not been gored in the bullring for the past ten years) was ignoble, and might represent women's menses because, he wrote, 'In sacrifice, sacrificial blood is distinguished from menstrual blood'. He talked about an exchange of victims, as with Abraham, with the animal replacing man as victim. Alchemical or magical terms appeared in his discussion of left and right. Leiris created a talented esoteric and archaistic atmosphere, unlike the extremely sound study by Marcel Mauss, who by drawing on the documented example of totemic societies declared that sacrifice had to have a socio-religious context. However, there is no socio-religious context for bullfighting. There is no devoutly maintained place of worship, there are no priests, no staunch believers, no consecrated sacrificial knife (only hunting weapons and weapons of war, which have nothing to do with sacrifice), no stake to bind the victim, no altar and no swift slitting of the bull's throat, which is an absolute no-no in bullfighting. Bullfighting does not belong to any bona fide socio-cultural system,[14] as demanded by Mauss, anthropology and common sense.[15] The *Miroir de la tauromachie* was nothing but a mirror decoy, a wonderfully written piece of fiction, but one that made reference to a reality soon described by Leiris himself as 'grotesque butchery'.[16]

In 1945 Leiris, who already had his doubts about bullfighting, nevertheless accepted Pierre Braunberger's offer to 'poetize' Lafront's technical text for a film that was considered a documentary on bullfighting. The writer took a great deal of trouble over a text in which he no longer had much belief, but the royalties on the 50,000 tickets sold in the first few weeks were very welcome in the difficult post-war climate. Leiris remained loyal to the publishers who printed his bullfighting texts, and his retractions, although courageous, were few and far between. 'Among other passionate enthusiasms that have coloured my life over the years, I have, therefore, finally eliminated my love for the *corrida* . . .';[17] 'It is no longer possible for me to make a tragedy out of bullfighting the way I did before and, now, what I notice first is the theatricality of most of the *toreros* and the absurdity of the heroic-aesthetic verbiage of their fans.'[18] Finally, his epitaph reveals more about his discovery of animal sensibility, a lesson he learned from his boxer dog: 'Here lies a reformed *aficionado* who valued canine friendship after enjoying the sight of bulls being spectacularly killed.'[19]

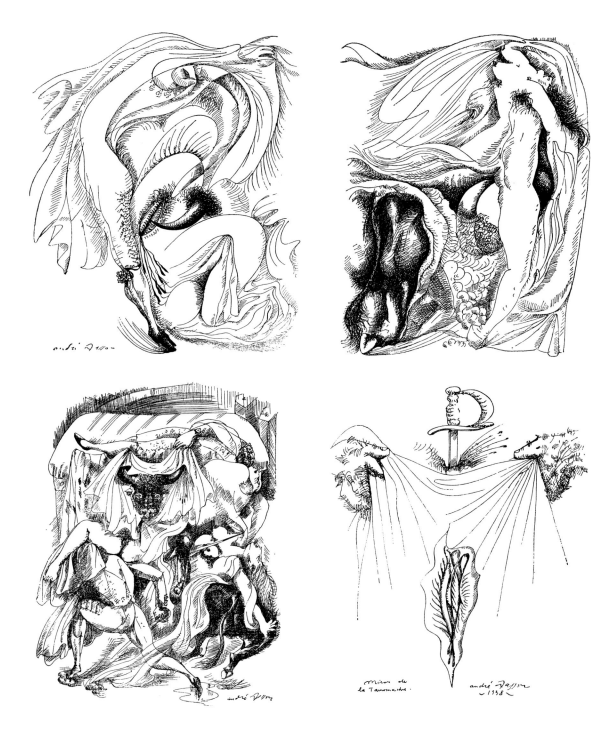

André Masson, illustrations for Michel Leiris, *Miroir de la Tauromachie* (1938).

A bronze statue of the French matador Nimeno II at Nîmes, 1994.

Timothy Mitchell, wearing his anthropologist's hat, conclusively dismantled the pseudo-scientific hypotheses that 'take the metaphor for the essence'.[20] He detected the contradictions in many of the arguments that appeared in the 1960s, particularly in Spain. The supposedly anthropological work of Julian Pitt-Rivers is surprisingly naive: 'The fact that this is a sacrifice seems so obvious that the anthropologist feels no need to justify it', or again 'The ordeal of the lance reveals the moral qualities of the victim [the bull] . . . which are essential from a ritual standpoint, since once sacrificed it [the victim] must bequeath them to humanity'.[21] Pitt-Rivers's mystic anthropocentrism attracted quite a following; one philosopher wrote: 'The bull places the value of its fight above that of its own suffering.'[22] Fairly often the bull is said to 'accept its suffering'. Even better, we learn that 'it delights in its intimate understanding with man; these two creatures who give themselves completely to each other in perfect equality attain a fulfilment close to love. The bull . . . attains a rest that is inaccessible without

A sacrificial death in the sand.

man, who signs it with death's initials, eternal rest.'[23]

In the field of bullfighting mysticism, Pitt-Rivers recalled that Diodorus of Sicily regarded the bull as sacred; this sacredness is secretly perpetuated in bullfighting. Pitt-Rivers decoded a mysterious reoccurrence of the number three in the bullring: three types of seats (*barreras, tendidos, gradas*); three roles (*sacrificado, sacrificador, sacrificante*); three participants (*toro, matador, publico*); three areas of the ring (*tablas, medios, callejon*); three kinds of creature (*hombres, caballos, toros*); three weapons (*varas, banderillas, muleta*); three actions (*citar, cargar, rematar*); three pairs of *banderillas* and, naturally, three *tercios*; three *peons*; three lines of participants (in the *paseo*). This return to a pseudo-science would have delighted a Renaissance would-be magus like Catherine de Médici, who had been deeply interested in an analogical decoding of the universe.

Even more incredible was the parallel that this anthropologist drew between Christ's actions at Calvary and those of the bull tortured in the village festivals of the Toro de la Vega in Torde-

sillas (Valladolid, Castilla la Vieja); this parallel was given as an example of counter-ritual.

A few inane examples will suffice. Christ entered Jerusalem by day; the bull enters Tordesillas by night. Christ walked up Calvary; the bull goes down to the place where it will be stabbed with lances. The executioners argued over Christ's tunic; the officiating immolators argue over the bull's physical attributes after killing it with a lance.[24] The Freudian theories circulated by Waldo Frank in *Virgin Spain* (1926), an American bestseller, rehabilitated Black Spain and presented bullfighting not as a drama of death, but of regeneration,[25] a theory that Hemingway called 'Freudian fiddle-faddle'. Waldo Frank exposed the transsexual metamorphoses of the matador, who is successively man and woman. This proponent of what Hemingway called 'erectile writing' also afforded an erotic interpretation of the wounds inflicted on the bull, particularly by the sword: 'sword interpenetration'. For a short time the blade held by the matador and embedded in the animal symbolizes the matador's penis, embedded 80 centimetres deep in the bull's body, so the animal would presumably be enjoying an intense orgasm. These examples are enough to reveal an interpretative spectrum that provides some insight into an obsessive sexual imagination.

ANTHROPOLOGY AND BULLFIGHTING

Around 1920 in Latin America there was re-newed interest in ancient Indian civilizations and their problems, tackled by five Nobel prize-winners for literature. Mexican muralism, like Russian Revolutionary art, provided a monumental repre-sentation of social life, although influenced heavily by its Indian past. Animals played no part here. In Peru, a major exhibition of popular art in 1939 by Alicia Bustamente provoked an interest that gave rise to the remarkable novel by Arguedas (1879–1946), in which the main hero is the bull in a bullfight. *Yawar Fiesta* (1941) was a 'blood festival'.[26] In July 1935 the author attended a so-called Indian bullfight in Puquio, a small rural city in the Andes, at which an Indian was killed.[27] Involved in Indian affairs from his downtrodden childhood, Arguedas was torn between his acute sympathy for the animals and a fondness for his Indian people, who represented 'uncorrupted humanity' despite their cruelty to animals.[28]

The story is this: the inhabitants of Puquio are divided over a festival, for some of the Creoles want a Spanish-style *corrida*, while the Indians want a blood festival. One Creole offers the Indians his finest bull, the wild and divine Misitu, which has to be brought down from the moun-tain. Paradoxically, the modernist ideologist Marxist party (APRA) from the neighbouring town supports the Spanish *corrida* of the colo-nialists in order to avoid the fatal accidents that often occurred at Indian festivals. Having been raised in an Indian-speaking culture, Arguedas' linguistic talents coupled with his knowledge of the area gave the incident an epic dimension and was peppered with facts: the festival was steeped in alcohol, a source of wealth for the Creoles; the Indian chief, who was the matador, was killed by the bull, which was bludgeoned to death by the Indians under the eyes of the real Spanish mata-dor, who was powerless to do anything. Like a nostalgic song that stirs the emotions, the beautiful prose denounces the injustices committed by the colonizers, as well as the impasse reached by the reformers, for whom the preservation of Indian traditions was a colonialist gambit designed to uphold slavery.

In this semi-imaginary, poetic situation, the bull festival became the iconic emblem of heroic resistance by innocent, oppressed peoples and of the authenticity of deep-rooted traditions in an unspoiled natural setting. The deification of the bull legalized its torture: the gods were made to be tortured. *Yawar fiesta* carried the bloody, drunken, accident-prone bull festivals into a powerful piece of poetic fiction. Arguedas turned an often squalid and always cruel reality into a seductive myth. Other extrapolations might posit bullfighting as a beneficial acculturation, which Fernando Matamoros on the contrary regarded as a 'Utopian mobilization of memory in order to legitimize domination' and 'a cultural hybridiza-tion that, as a last resort, conceals the primordial disaster of the ethnocide-genocide of the Indian peoples.'[29] Arguedas' other novels make virtually no mention of bullfighting. Full of conflicting contradictions and possibly compromised politi-cally by his wife, he committed suicide in the grounds of his university.

In 1966 Arguedas' literary friend, the journal-ist Augusto Goicochea Luna, provided an account of the many variations on the patronage festivals held in 'the backbone of the Andes': in one place, they ripped the heads off live geese suspended from a rope (*Jalapato*) while onlookers roared with laughter; in another, an inferior matador was hired in Lima; and in yet another, bulls fought each other. One festival for St Peter, patron of fishermen, was held just for family, with no strangers allowed, in Chalhuanca, on the road out of Abancay – a fishing village in the south of Peru – in a makeshift arena. A massive condor was dragged in by its wings, accompanied by a dancer disguised as a condor with an enormous beak, who mimicked the bird's desperate movements. The viscera of a freshly killed donkey had attracted the bird, whose legs were grabbed by a hunter hiding in the donkey's stomach. The musicians and dancers in the arena fled at the appearance of the first bull, covered with an *enjalma* and with coins fastened between the horns, which *aficionados* tried to grab. A drunkard was caught by the bull, the women screamed in terror. The *aficionados* tried to grab the coins. A child succeeded but his thigh was pierced through.

The entrance of an enormous bull caused a mad rush. The condor perched on the bull's *morillo* was struggling desperately, as if it were trying to keep its balance on the animal's back. 'People noticed with amazement that the condor had been sewn to the bull's hide . . . its talons were trapped in the *morillo* at which it pecked desperately . . . A trickle of hot blood flowed down the legs of the bull, which was bellowing with rage and pain.' A matador requested a sword and a curved sabre (*alfanje*). In an awed silence, he threw the *muleta* at the head of the bull, which he then killed with a sword blow to the neck (*bajonazo*). The bull fell to the ground, its legs in the air. The helpers immobilized the condor, whose talons were freed by cutting the

hide of the bull. A man brought a cobbler's awl (a thick, curved needle), the women pitied the condor, 'poor little old man', while an assistant put out the bird's eyes with the sharp point. The bird trembled, its convulsions increased, and it was thrown into the air; it wailed grievously. 'Hundreds of eyes followed this fatal flight, the king of open spaces rose into the air', but 'fell back to earth further away', killing itself.

In other festivals in *Yawar Fiesta*, the condor pecked out the eyes of the bull, or broke open the frontal bone, then the crowd battered it to death with sticks, fighting over the eyes and feathers as amulets against misfortune. An English-speaking newspaper begged readers to stop one spectacle of this sort, in which the bird had been intoxicated with alcohol.[30]

There were echoes of bullfighting in this event, such as the *bajonazo* (a low *estocada*), and of hunting, such as the capturing of the condor, while the dancers in the ring, the orchestra, the unexpected appearance of the bull and a mime were all reminiscent of a carnival. The danger of these games was doubled by the condor, which was temporarily the bull's ally against the men. The weapons were makeshift: stones and oranges thrown by the assistants, the awl used to sew the bird's feet in the living hide of the bull, and, above all, the weapon that was the condor, which was pitted both against the bull and the participants.

The eye was of paramount importance in this story: the spectators' eyes and those of the bull, enucleated by the bird. The condor's eyes that became amulets, testifying to the power of the victim, the bull being regarded merely as a 'condor-bearer'. The narrator witnessing these things deplored the perverse nature of the 'fiesta

A condor at the *Yawar Fiesta*, Peru.

brava . . . through a fanatical *afición* for Indianity, in those distant regions in the southern Andes.'

BATAILLE AND SADE ON THE TERRACES

Around 1920 Georges Bataille was just a brilliant graduate from the École des Chartres, working at the Bibliothèque Nationale de France and under-going psychoanalysis by Dr Adrien Borel, who helped him to discover some 'heavy obsessional material'.[31] Bataille dared to describe this material in a story, which he could not publish under his own name and which formed the point of departure for his entire output. In a similar way to Baudelaire, who was fascinated by decaying carcasses, Bataille was obsessed with excrement. Bataille's novella, *Histoire de l'œil* (*Story of the Eye*) appeared in 1928 under the pseudonym of 'Lord Auch', which meant Lord to the Shithouse ('Auch' being a shortened form of *aux chiottes*, French slang for toilet). In *Histoire de l'œil*, the distinguished Englishman, Lord Edmund, is a voyeur, a wealthy purveyor of erotic, bizarre, dramatic or even criminal scenarios, offered to his trio of companions for their intense sexual pleasure.[32] Bullfighting was the catalyzing event for Bataille's obsessions, the driving force behind the book and, in several pages it forms the central and seminal element in Bataille's discovery of obscenity. The heroine, Simone, prefers bull-fighting to a pigsty where a prostitute screams erotic ravings: 'Sir Edmund deployed his ingenuity at providing us with obscene spectacles at random, but Simone still preferred bullfights.'

For Bataille, as for Max Ernst, Victor Brauner or the filmmaker Luis Buñuel, the eyeball was an object of fantasy that recalled the mythic oedipal enucleation. It also informed a large part of Bataille's life as a teenager, when his father, after going into decline, went blind. There are several eyeballs in *L'Histoire de l'œil*: a young dead woman's glassy wide-open eyes, on which Simone urinates, or the eye of the priest whom the trio have just murdered. The central episode of 22 May 1922 occurs at the moment when the matador, Granero, dies after being gored in the eye with a horn, an event that cannot actually have been seen by Bataille or the spectators, who would have read about it in the newspapers. Sir

Salvador Dalí, *Tauromachie surréaliste: La Tauromachie individuelle (reworking by the artist of the printed poster announcing the bullfight held in his honour)*, 1961, paint over printed paper.

Edmund arranged the testicles of the last bull killed by Granero on a plate. Bataille then described the virtual, sordid exchange that took place between the eye expelled from Granero's head, his death, and Simone's act of putting the testicles in her vagina at the exact point when the tragedy (Granero's death) gave her such an intense climax that she lost consciousness:

> The events that followed were without transition or connection, not because they weren't actually related, but because my attention was so absent as to remain absolutely dissociated. In just a few seconds: first, Simone bit into one of the raw balls, to my dismay; then Granero advanced towards the bull, waving his scarlet cloth; finally, almost at once, Simone with a blood-red face and a suffocating lewdness, uncovered her long white thighs up to her moist vulva, into which she slowly and surely fitted the second pale globule . . . Granero was thrown back by the bull and wedged against the balustrade; the horns struck the balustrade three times at full speed; at the third blow, one horn plunged into the right eye and through the head. A shriek of unmeasured horror coincided with a brief orgasm for Simone, who was lifted up from the stone seat only to be flung back with a bleeding nose, under a blinding sun; men instantly

rushed over to haul away Granero's body, the right eye dangling from the head . . . Thus two globes of equal size and consistency had suddenly been propelled in opposite directions at once. One, the white ball of the bull, had been thrust into the 'pink and dark' cunt that Simone had bared to the crowd; the other, a human eye, had spurted from Granero's head with the same force as a bundle of innards from a belly. This coincidence, tied to death and to a sort of urinary liquefaction of the sky, first brought us back . . .

Bataille was not the pleasure-seeking sex maniac denounced by Sartre. He had bought and published the manuscript of the *Cent vingt journées de Sodome* (1930),[33] saw Sade as a victim of violence and, with Sade, he made a terrifying revelation about human nature. Bataille's transgressive obscenity 'forces us to go against ourselves and beyond ourselves'. The writer-prophet reveals a human capacity for violence that, although unsuspected, hidden and denied,[34] is actually borne out by bullfighting, pending the onset of war. Sexual pleasure caused by the sight of torture is a perversion that could well be unique to man. Like Sade, Bataille had not been deceived in choosing a bullfight as the central episode of *L'Histoire de l'œil*. Bataille's obscenity was transgressive, unlike the delectable eroticism of the *Corrida du Premier mai* by a worldly Cocteau,[35] which was pleasantly arranged and accepted by the kind complicity of an animal deeply honoured to please mankind: 'The beast adorns itself with a bouquet of hollyhocks and a mantle of blood, as if flaunting its pride as it accepts death.'

With Nietzsche, Bataille placed man at the other end of the spectrum to the glorious matador, who is incompatible with Judeo-Christian man,

created in God's image. Paradoxically, the bull emerged from the arena the victor, because its lack of considered cruelty set it apart from human brutality. A fan of bullfighting, Bataille was nevertheless touched by the words of his friend Maurice Heine, who ate 'sparingly so as to feed numerous cats' and who, like Sade, expressed such a dislike of the death penalty that he 'even solemnly condemned bullfighting'.[36] Elsewhere, Bataille provided a wonderful description of the mystery of animals:

> For, not being simply a thing, the animal is not closed and inscrutable to us. The animal opens before me a depth that attracts me and is familiar to me. In a sense, I know this depth: it is my own. It is also that which is farthest removed from me, that which deserves the name depth, which means precisely *that which is unfathomable to me.*[37]

No one could go further than Georges Bataille in the demystification of both bullfighting and human nature. It is therefore hardly surprising that 'Lord Auch', as soon as he was identified, should have been evicted from the terraces as a troublemaker.

Bullfighting poster from Acapulco, Mexico.

nine

In the Twentieth Century

Mexico's isolation from Europe favoured a distinctive style of bullfighting, and the number of bullfights held there soared from 124 in 1937 to 215 in 1955.[1] Famous matadors included Armillita Chico (1911–1978), who succeeded Gaona (1888–1975). The situation gradually changed and, in 1944, Ruiz Camino Arruza (born 1920) went back to Spain to fight bulls. Luis Procuna (1923–1995) played himself in Buñuel's biopic, which was awarded a prize in Venice in 1956 and did not show bullfighting in a particularly favourable light.[2] Since 1970 Mexican matadors have not been highly rated by French *aficionados*, although French *toreros* have had profitable winter seasons in Latin America. Nimeno II (born 1954) confirmed his *alternativa* in 1979 in Mexico City and was a triumphant success in 1987 in Venezuela; 120 of his 416 bullfights took place on the other side of the Atlantic.

After the 1940s the construction of bullrings in Latin America peaked twice, around 1950 and around 1980.[3] In Mexico a variety of different spectacles were held in the 493 temporary arenas and 217 permanent arenas, including dances, boxing matches and *jaripeo* horsemanship. The *charreria*, a national spectacle, required the use of a *lienzo de charro* or Mexican horsemanship arena. Arenas with a seating capacity of 3,000,

which were often temporary, were built near railway stations. Every year, 704 *novilladas*-A used *toros de casta* (bulls bred for bullfighting) while 1,782 *novilladas*-B used fattening cattle, which meant that these spectacles were not all that different from slaughtering for food. Half the 215 formal bullfights were held in five states. The state of Jalisco and the arena in Guadalajara held the most bullfights (475 spectacles, 25 bullfights, 70 *novilladas*-A, 380 *novilladas*-B). Yucatan specialized in *novilladas*-B (288). Oaxaca, the homeland of Benito Juarez, was traditionally anti-bullfighting. State taxes on admission tickets were around 13 per cent. Bullrings were to be found near sports facilities (in Vera Cruz, in Mexico City and in Matamoros), in tourist, colonial or historic towns (Orisaba), near airports, in farming cities (Leon) and near fairs (Tijuana, 21,000 seats).

Some of the arenas were vast in size and ambition, a reflection of the passion for bullfighting. The Plaza Monumental bullring in Mexico City, which was inaugurated by El Soldado, Luis Procuna and Manolete, remained open throughout the year, maintained by teams of technicians. The first world broadcast of episodes of a bullfight was televised live on 4 October 1946. There were daily bullfighting programmes on the radio between 1 pm and 4 pm and around 10 pm, and

Devil bullfighters in a papercut depicting the Mexican 'Day of the Dead', 1980s.

these programmes broadcast weekend bullfights live, from 7 pm to midnight.

Setbacks occurred immediately. The bankrupt promoter Neguib Simon died so insolvent that his corpse almost ended up in a common grave. The matador Gaona, in his capacity as administrator, came up against the tax system and a growing lack of interest, while the maintenance costs for the building remained exorbitant. The temporary closures became seasonal. Rafael Herrerías acquired the management for $3,000,000 in 1993, and the bullring made losses of around $15,000,000 in eight years. The seats were only filled erratically when the bullfighting idols performed there: on 23 July 2000, at the beginning of one season, only one in ten seats was taken; impresario Rafael Herrerías refused to allow any veterinary inspection and even banned the use of a *novilla* (young cow) to prevent it.[4] Out of the 22 million inhabitants in the federal district, between 8,000 and 15,000 people attended a bullfight in 2000 and 2001. In 2008 the Plaza Monumental bullring gave away one seat for every 478 inhabitants in the District of Mexico City, fewer than in France (one seat for 314 inhabitants). The verdict of the French *afición* was blunt: 'the organization managing La Monumental is connected with other companies in the same financial group and cares very little about the quality of the bullfight. You could almost be at a second-rate *feria* in France or Spain'.[5]

Carved wooden figurines forming a bullfighting scene, 1980s, Mexico.

Mexican society
women at a bullfight,
1910s.

Cover for a Mexican book
of plays, *A Bullfight – or
Luisa's Love, c.* 1910.

Latin American cattle-breeding was temporarily brought to a halt by the aphthous fever (1946, 1952), and then affected by the first air transport of cows (1950) and the introduction of artificial insemination around 1974. The agrarian reforms of 1910, particularly those in Cardenas in Mexico of 1934–40, as well as urban growth (from 30 to 45 per cent in 1950), had less of an impact on ranches than expected. The large Mexican bullring owners included ranches, chains of restaurants and hotels in their property portfolios.[6] By way of an example, Tlaxcala, 200 km from Mexico City, was well documented, and there were around ten *toro bravo* ranches there in 1937 and thirteen in 1955.[7] In 1976, the most famous Piedras Negras ranch was selling between 50 and 70 bulls per year to various bullrings, including the Plaza Monumental. In 1991,[8] half the 34 owners of ranches breeding fighting bulls were working at a skilled trade in Mexico City; the *toro bravo* serves as a mark of identity, but it is very expensive, because ranches need 60 cows and three stud bulls for breeding; fighting

Poster for Rancho Aguilar, Tlaxcala, Mexico.

bulls live for four years, whereas fattening cattle are killed after ten to eighteen months. In 1991 there were 250 private ranches in Mexico. In 1999 only 20 of the 320 breeder members of the Mexican Association were supplying bulls for the bullfights,[9] so contrary to what the breeders say, bullfighting has a very limited economic impact on cattle ranches, most of which are diversifying their production.

The Colombian artist Fernando Botero painted his *Corrida* in France when at the height of his powers (1984, around the age of 50). His opulent style was reminiscent of Renoir and Picasso. The wealth of detail in his paintings was comparable to the renowned posters by Carlos Ruano Llopis (1879–1950), who settled in Mexico City around 1930. Not everything is oversized in Botero's bullring, neither the structure nor the spectators are exaggerated, and the bull even less so than the people. The actual size of the tiny accessories (the buckle on the picador's gaiters) is enough to point up the exaggeration. Even though Botero actually wore a matador's costume when painting, he was less than accurate when depicting a picador wounding a bull bristling with *banderillas* and his matador does not plunge the sword *en la cruz*.

FERNANDO BOTERO

Botero's *Corrida* is also a 'story of the eye', but not that of Lord Auch. Botero (born 1932 in Medellín, Colombia) explained to Jean Cau that 'the artist watches the bullfight, which is itself observed by the spectators'.[10] Canetti also stated that, in the bullring, 'Wherever one looks, one meets eyes'.[11] The animal's eyes sparkle, while the human gaze is dull, bearing down on a matador who is holding an apple in his hand like a symbolic eyeball. *Le Bigleur* is a cross-eyed matador. The poor horse is blindfolded, and the bull is glaring at the matador, who is brandishing the ear which has just been cut from the living animal.[12] The crowd in the terraces, literally 'black with people', simultaneously

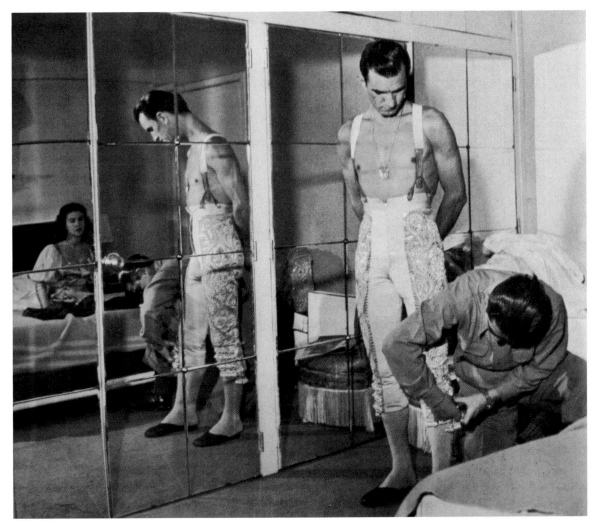

Gisèle Freund, *The Torero Carlos Arruza Getting Dressed*, Mexico City, 1950.

resembles mourners at the funeral for those already lifeless beings, so that death hovers over the terraces more visibly than in the bullring. There are burnt-out cigarette stubs – emblems of death – everywhere. Matador Luis Chalmeta can ascend to heaven because he is inflated like a balloon. Conversely, the picador and his horse standing heavily in the ring look like an equestrian statue from the Italian Renaissance, a period of art that was a frequent source of inspiration for Botero; they represent eternity and permanence, thereby halting the ravages of time; Botero's picador believes himself to be immortal. Botero is therefore painting death in this bullfight. He claims to be transforming the bullfight 'into a still-life: only the spectators filing past the canvas are alive'.[13] Did Botero know, like Hemingway who described them, that corpses swell up? In

Pablo Picasso, *The Bullring*, 1901, pastel.

Botero's bullfights, the keen eye of the bull looks on, and intelligence and life swap sides.

HEMINGWAY

Ernest Hemingway (1899–1961) lived and breathed death and violence towards animals. For a time he lived in Spanish-speaking Cuba and introduced bullfighting to (virtually) every continent, through his novels and the films they inspired. From birth, he was subjected to a rare and insidious type of psychological violence.

His mother forced him into a false twinhood with his sister, who was 16 months older, resulting in a feminization that lasted beyond adolescence. His father, a powerless bystander, tried to boost Ernest's masculinity by teaching him to kill animals. Hemingway, like Leiris, took refuge in writing. His novels reveal the various stages of his inner turmoil.[14] His antidotes included drugs, alcohol, sex and, above all, a fascination with any kind of violent death, human or animal. A war reporter on the Italo-Austrian front at

Fernando Botero, *Juan Rodriguez Conejo*, 1988, oil on canvas.

Fernando Botero, *Woman in the Bullring*, 1992, oil on canvas.

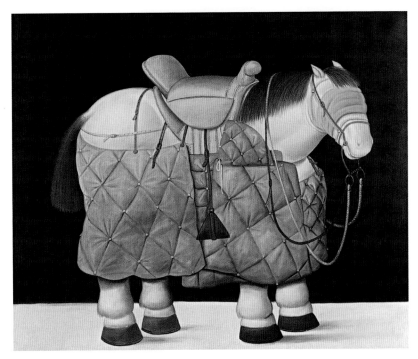

Fernando Botero, *The Horse of a Picador*, 1992, oil on canvas.

Rosendo Rodriguez, *Bullfight*, 20th century, painted clay sculpture.

the age of nineteen, he gathered corpses mutilated by an explosion. He was attracted by the harsh beauty of Spain: 'there is no other country in the world like Spain'.[15] He believed in the myth of its savagery. It was actually in Paris, in conversations with the writer Gertrude Stein, that Hemingway first became interested in bullfighting.[16] After 1918, 'the only place where you could see life and death, *i.e.,* violent death now that the wars were over, was in the bullring'.[17]

One of Hemingway's first bullfighting texts, a story about the San Firmín Festival in Pamplona, published in the *Toronto Star* (20 October 1923), preceded *The Sun Also Rises* (1926), which lends the bulls of Pamplona a mythic power. According to Gertrude Stein, Hemingway had a 'truly sensitive capacity for emotion', but he had thrown it away when 'he became obsessed with sex and violent death'.[18] After the San Isidro bullfighting festival in Madrid, which marked the retirement of Belmonte (1929), Hemingway made the most

of the success of *A Farewell to Arms* to begin *Death in the Afternoon,* which he finished in 1932. His 115 bullfights, his kills on safari, his hunting and big-game fishing were an obsession. He was in his element as a correspondent in the Spanish Civil War for the Republicans and covered the taking of Teruel with Robert Capa (March to May 1938). During the military operations, Franco husbanded the Andalusian ranches to the maximum; around 20 breeders were massacred by the Republicans who, like their socialist predecessors, denounced the capitalization of land for bulls: 'One less *torero*, one less fascist', read the *ABC* in 1938.[19]

On 24 May 1939 the Victory Bullfight in the packed Madrid bullring was the apotheosis of all political bullfights. The *muletas* of the matadors, Lalanda, Ortega and Bienvenida, bore the words *Arriba España* (Long Live Spain), and the air rang with Spanish and Falangist anthems. A friend of the former French ambassador in Spain, Franco treated Philippe Pétain to a mockery of a bullfight in September 1942, held at the packed Vélodrome d'Hiver in Paris, less than two months after the appalling round-up of the Jews on 16 July 1942.[20]

The Italians proved to be more dignified by boycotting the bullfight ordered by Mussolini for May 1923 in Milan, featuring the matador Pajerito. Most of the matadors rallied to Franco. In receipt of substantial tax advantages, they grew wealthy and some, like Paquirri later, were allegedly supporters of Opus Dei.[21]

Violence in the bullring represented an attempt to gloss over the violence of the dictatorship, but Hemingway, living in Cuba in 1939, was keen to ignore the pro-Franco success of the bullfight. He wrote *For Whom The Bell Tolls*, in which all references to bullfighting seem an integral part of every Spaniard's life. He sold his screenplay for a film with Ingrid Bergman and Gary Cooper, which contributed greatly to his prestige and wealth in the USA. Hemingway's films consolidated

Ernest Hemingway with the bullfighter Antonio Ordonez, c. 1950s.

Ernest Hemingway (in white trousers) facing the bull during the Pamplona bull-run, 1924.

Bulls racing into the ring at Pamplona.

Bullfight poster, Tarifa, 2005.

the link between the United States and Mexico with regard to bullfighting. Hollywood played an important role, since the exchange of films with Latin America was a political decision of Franklin Roosevelt, who organized the State Department's Office of the Coordinator of Inter-American Affairs, created to promote friendly relations between American neighbours.[22]

Death in the Afternoon (1932), a sort of catechism for bullfighting, did not go down very well with the critics on publication, but Hemingway's publisher, Maxwell Perkins, saw the book for what it was: 'The book piles upon you wonderfully, and becomes to one reading it – who at first thinks bullfighting only a small matter – immensely important'.[23] In fact, anyone with the patience to read the seemingly dogmatic prose in this book will discover many facts about bullfighting, for example, confirmation of the similarities between bullfighting and public executions involving torture. In the post-war period, the technical information contained in *Death in the Afternoon* satisfied a demand for documentary information. It also advanced a Catholic standpoint: the animal, with no soul, is at man's disposal, like any material; it is 'the marble a sculptor cuts'.[24] Against the shocked English concept of 'fair play', he offset the dangers involved in the fight, the 'philosophy of heroism'. He claimed that the animal was killed as humanely as possible; he rejected the use of the *puntilla* and claimed that 'this repugnant business was made unnecessary by the invention of the volapié',[25] which was an obvious lie. The Americans knew nothing about bullfighting and the book became the tourists' bible in Spain.[26]

Hemingway is an emblematic representative of the *aficionados* who were in love with death. In Seville, following serious injury to the matador

José Luis Vargas in the ring, the admission price went up by 35 per cent (various *aficionados* commented 'if we had known what was going to happen, we would have paid top price').[27] Many people with suicidal tendencies who 'find life only in death'[28] are attracted by bullfighting, like Hemingway, Montherlant, Leiris, the poet Alain Borne, the matador Belmonte, the artist and *aficionado* Bernard Buffet, as well as the heroine in the film *Hable con Ella* (*Talk to Her*), by Almodóvar, who depicts a type of Russian roulette bullfight: kneeling in front of the gate of the *toril* to wait for the bull. The fate of El Nimeno II reflected this climate: admired as a *torero*, neglected after being severely injured, he found that a second career was not an option; abandoned to his 'mental, physical and financial difficulties', he committed suicide on 25 November 1991.[29]

FRANCIS BACON

This anguish of being trapped in a death-dealing system was wonderfully expressed by the London-based Irish painter Francis Bacon (1909–1992),[30] who devoted one of his triptychs to bullfighting. The use of this religious-seeming form for this work, dedicated to the murdered poet Lorca, imbued it with mysticism. As is often the case with Bacon's work, this painting places the main character, here the bull, in dramatic isolation, transforming the living animal into a butchery product. The fate shared by meat, animal and man was an obsession in Bacon's work: 'we are meat, we are potential carcasses'.

Bacon denounced the inconsistency of people. 'You can think of the whole horror of life – of one thing living off another. It's like all those stupid things that are said about bull-fighting. Because people will eat meat and then complain about bull-fighting; they will go in and complain

Francis Bacon, *Study for Bullfight, no. 2*, 1969, oil on canvas.

about bull-fighting covered with furs and with birds in their hair'.[31] Some of his sketches for the bullfight show a matador and a bull, merged into one, clearly identified by the red colour of the *burladero* (wooden shield in front of the *barrera*), marked with a number. Bacon was the only artist powerful enough to express the distress caused by the imprisonment of a terrified animal searching for a way out.

FRANCE AFTER 1945

After the end of World War Two in 1945, the French threw themselves into eating and entertainment. They were prepared to believe everything in order to forget everything;[32] it was as if the human race was taking revenge on animals for its own inhumanity. Bullfighting seemed to be an unmissable spectacle for the French seeking the Spanish sun. By an incredible coincidence, all the key posts in the French news industry had been given to *aficionados*. *Le Temps*, closed down for collaboration with the Nazis during the War, became *Le Monde*, which kept the same sports reporter, who was a bullfighting fan. From 1962 onwards Jean Lacouture presented his remarkable documentary research with a dramatic flair that made his accounts eminently believable and encouraged people to believe that a matador was killed at every bullfight! There were other coincidences: Hélène Gordon, who became an *aficionada* in the company of Michel Leiris, married Pierre Lazareff, director of the leading Paris publishing group, and founded the magazine *Elle*, which supported bullfighting, along with its rival *Marie-Claire*, edited by Marcelle Auclair. From *Le Canard Enchaîné* to *Paris-Match*, and from the communist *Humanité* to the conservative *Figaro*, the reassuring disinformation about bullfighting over the past 50 years reduced the muzzled, caricatured opposition to scornful silence. Club Méditerranée distributed tickets to bullfights. Spanish exiles, nostalgic for Spain, lent their support to the French bullfights, betraying Republican opposition to bullfighting. Around 1963 there was an influx of bullfighting fans from Islamic Algeria, a country that was anti bullfighting. Repatriates like Camille Lapierre or Vincent Bourg became popular bullfight journalists.

Pierre Braunberger's film *La Course de taureaux, images, animées* (1951) was passed off as a documentary, although he was more misleading than he was informative, for example stating that the recently discovered Lascaux cave paintings were forerunners of bullfighting. The tedious technical litany spoken by Auguste Lafront was illustrated by skilful montages that reduced the bull to a simple interchangeable mechanism, a robot-bull, formed by an invisible collage of several beasts; the film's huge success[33] immediately drew an audience of 50,000. The Catholic Church added its moralistic pennyworth. The famous Dominican preacher Father Sertillanges proclaimed that 'having regrets about animal sacrifice is a sin'; here he was following in the footsteps of the Jesuit Julian Pereda,[34] who said that 'the reason animals exist is man' and that there was no cruelty in the bullring. As soon as he arrived in Nîmes, Monseigneur Cadilhac declared to the magazine *Corrida*:[35] 'The current relationship between the Church and bullfighting . . . is a good relationship.' This prelate may have influenced the modification of the Code of Canon Law (1983), which removed the word 'bullfight' from Article 285, and completely ruled out any legal discussion. His successor in Nîmes, Monseigneur Wattbled, made reference to this law. He allowed the *aficionado* municipality to loan him the bullring for his consecration (*sacre* in French), which opponents called the '*mas-sacre*'. He did not attend bullfights, but donations from the Catholics in Nîmes were made to the Art et Foi Association, which organized a Bullfighting Colloquium (11 December 2005). This organization paid for some eminent *aficionados* to attend the event, under the presidency of *aficionado* Abbé Jacques Teissier, whose militant texts, illustrated with photos of bullfights, were featured for a long time on the site of the Conférence des Évêques de France (2004), which pretended to withdraw them (2006) in the face of public protests.

At one of the first post-War exhibitions, Picasso initiated heated arguments when he exhibited his bicycle saddle transformed into a *Bull's Head*. A simple permutation of the parts of a bicycle evoked both the animal and the bull-fighter's training *carretón* (fake bull). Cubist artists, who had showed no great interest in the

bullring, did produce several portraits of matadors, notably those by Gris and Mirò. Picasso
abandoned his erotic, mythical bullfights of 1930
and revived his abandoned plan to illustrate the
treatise by Pepe-Hillo with 26 aquatints (1957).[36]
Profoundly inspired on his way back from a
bullfight in Arles, he spent just four days outlin-
ing the gangling silhouettes of the bullfight in his
Toros y toreros, many of which were realized in
sepia ink.[37]

The irresistible gaiety of Picasso's drawings
for *Toros y toreros* was reminiscent of Daumier's
Don Quichottes, albeit a little more comical and
a little less profound. These drawings were widely
reproduced on crockery; tons of meat have been
devoured on plates produced by Vallauris. Their
playful appearance, completely divorced from
reality, is in keeping with the euphoric mood of
this period.

ten

Modern Times

Around 1945, the legal status of bullfighting in France was still governed by the law of 2 July 1850 (the so-called Loi Grammont), which made it an offence to maltreat animals, whether they were domestic, tamed or kept in captivity.[1] The *afición* proposed one exception, legalizing bull-fights in towns where they had already existed illegally in France since 1853. At the Conseil de la République, the opponents of bullfighting, who were ridiculed, uninformed (some did not even know that the mattress-like protection for horses, the *peto*, existed) and very much in the minority, accepted a paragraph they believed harmless, which is now Paragraph 4 of Article 521 of the Penal Code: 'The law (Grammont) does not apply to bullfights when an unbroken tradition can be cited.' The Deputies voted more or less unanimously for this exception, which they believed to be conciliatory.[2]

In French law, this exception is contrary to Article 1 of the Constitution, which ensures 'the equality of all citizens before the law . . . without distinction of origin'. Taking the criterion of geographical location as a criterion of penaliza-tion is a type of racism, partly defined by habitat. Since cruelty is lawful in Nîmes and the enowned bullfighting areas, its opposite, the protection of bulls, appears unlawful. The so-called 'tradition' of cruelty in the South of France is defamatory to

those southerners who defend animals and who are now looking set to become the vast majority.

French case law shows that the notion of an 'unbroken tradition' has been taken to ridiculous extremes by judicial authorities with a historical love of bullfighting. No one could have foreseen that certain judgments might turn out to be a travesty; accordingly, in Pau, in 2001, a ruling stated that 'the concept of a bullfighting tradition should not be confused with a tradition of organiz-ing bullfights nor should it be restricted to it, given that the latter is in actual fact merely just one expression of it, since a tradition cannot be reduced to just one of its material and external manifesta-tions'. In other words, 'material and external manifestations', such as a dream, a poem or a discussion, might be enough to start a tradition.[3]

France has therefore become the preferred hunting ground of the Spanish impresarios. The brilliant Balañà (born 1883) was the first large-scale impresario and he founded a dynasty. Balañà contributed to the growth of bullfighting in France when he settled in Marseille in 1936, during the Republican ban on bullfighting in Spain. After returning to Barcelona following Franco's seizure of power, he launched the careers of Chamaco and Litri, created their brand image, bribed the newspapers and paid the matadors a percentage of the takings. The launch of El

The famous bull-fighter Manolete (right) at Camara in 1945, two years before his fatal goring at Linares.

Cordobés in France generated a monumental publicity ladder, one that took in film, television and a giant image on the Eiffel Tower. In 2005 the Choperita dynasty – a Spanish family involved in every aspect of the staging of *corridas* – consolidated the system, strengthening the technical team and acquiring the monopoly on the Las Ventas bullring in Madrid. According to Hemingway, the impresario 'can make his subordinates slaves',[4] a situation that matadors dislike even more than the danger inherent in the ring. The percentage of matadors killed compared to the number of bulls slaughtered in official bullfights, estimated at 0.0021 in 1995, has dropped even further. Fortunately, dicing with death is now more likely to be a simple turn of phrase than a tragic extreme. Eight injuries in the bullring in France in 2005 (out of 140 events) that required hospitalization were treated by the numerous doctors in the Congrès de l'Association Française de Chirurgie Taurine (AFCT), who are hardly likely to be overworked.

MODERN MATADORS

Starting a career as a matador is not easy, anywhere. All young *toreros* must buy their bull to appear in public. A celebrity bullfighter might perform in 1,500 bullfights in the course of a career. Winter contracts in South America double the profits. A celebrity *torero* can earn seven to eight million euros per season, like footballers; in Mexico, $150,000 can be earned per session and, for one-off bullfights, between $120,000 (Enrique Ponce, 1999) and $150,000 (El Juli, 1999). Television increases the wages six or sevenfold. A well-liked *torero* can earn around 8,000 euros per bullfight while a picador receives 760 euros. They pay out: between 1,500 and 2,404 euros for a suit of lights, 762 euros for a cape and 2,287 euros for a sword.[5]

Some matadors became the stuff of legend. Certain novels outdid each other with their flights of fancy: Marc Roumengou analysed the plot construction in five French and Spanish books (1934 to 1963) about Manolete, whose death in

Conchita Citron killing a bull.

the bullring, in 1947, made the news all over the world.[6] Promoted to the rank of *Caliph*, addicted to whisky and cocaine, afflicted with Addison's disease, the matador was transformed by the five authors into five different heroes. Conversely, in the film *Matador* (1986), Almodóvar depicted a murdering, necrophiliac *torero*, whose perversions are submerged by a dazzling whirl of images.

Celebrity matadors like César Rincón, the national hero of Colombia, often became breeders; but the *toreros* did not cut such a dash in politics: Simon Casas failed in his own constituency of Gard with only 2,078 votes out of 83,134 voters.[7]

However, a few matadors, showing more courage than they ever did in the bullring, have denounced the cruelty of a spectacle that they afterwards abandoned. Antonio Moreno, who

had been a child prodigy as a nine-year-old matador, realized, at the age of 30, that killing afforded a sadistic pleasure. Now a vegetarian, he denounced the Catholic Church's support for bullfighting and the public funding of the event. One day, the Colombian matador, Àlvaro Mùnera, saw a kneeling bull 'weeping' after four *estocadas*. Injured and hospitalized in Spain, Mùnera received criticism that opened his eyes to his thoughtlessness. As a member of the Town Council in Medellín, he went on to campaign for animal rights and the abolition of bullfighting.[8]

MODERN BULLS

Four-year-old fighting bulls cost 2,500 euros. European subsidies for breeders are 220 euros per year, per bull.[9] In Spain, each of the 338 breeders of fighting bulls, in 528 ranches, supply a maximum of eighteen bulls to the bullrings each year (on average); in Portugal, there are 26 self-styled bullfighting ranches. In 2001, 309 ranches provided the 5,335 bulls that were killed (all spectacles) in Europe.[10] In France 4 breeders in 38 ranches are situated in the triangle formed by Fréjus, Arles and Béziers. During the course of 106 French spectacles in 2008 (68 bullfights, 636 bulls killed in all spectacles), 16 per cent of breeders were French.[11]

Bulls often collapse spontaneously in the bull-ring, a problem that started bedevilling bullfights around 1975. When faced with completely disabled beasts, the matadors, according to fans, 'become their nurses and the disaster a habit'.[12] In Madrid, as *El País* lamented, 'They are not bulls but kittens'.[13] There are various reasons for this: the lance, illegally placed at the back of the *morillo* may strike the spinal column and the rachidian nerves. Various ranches, now involved in intensive ranching, may suddenly start over-feeding the animals over the six months prior to a bullfight and give them injections of anabolic steroids, either hormonal or chemical, such as Clenbuterol. The skeleton is overburdened by the muscle mass, control becomes difficult and copious lactic acid causes paralysis.[14] In France, despite the evidence as to its causes, the Institut National de la Recherche Agronomique will receive 103,600 euros to study the reasons for the falls of 50 to 60 bulls. Two-thirds of the money is to be paid by the French INRA,

Eugenio Lucas Villamil, *The Bullfight* c. 1890s.

An inevitable end.

their living from products other than bulls and would more or less continue doing the same work without the latter. In Spain, they benefit from 30 million euros of direct subsidies, which could be used to improve their farms, and indirect subsidies for schools, fan clubs and marketing.

In every bullfighting country on both continents, the loss-making bullfights could not continue without public subsidies paid by the taxpayers, in Spain estimated at 530 million euros of direct and indirect aid. In 2006 the cost of a bullfight in Spain was 25,000 euros, a third of which was subsidized by the town councils. Only the large bullrings (loss-making and subsidized, like Nîmes) make the impresarios fabulously rich, since they are paid handsomely with public money by the town councils.[18] In Spain, television broadcasts of bullfights by a Spanish public channel represent a loss of 50 million euros. The Greens are incensed that a spectacle 'where an animal is so badly maltreated that it dies, should be subsidized to the detriment of genuinely cultural activities, like the theatre'.[19] Mediterranean opponents of bullfighting take photographs of small empty bullrings, which the *Echo de Céret* has bravely suggested should be closed: these small French bullrings, which have proliferated since incessant lawsuits have been lost by anti-bullfighting campaigners due to judges turning a blind eye, are never filled, despite numerous seats being given away free to mask the financial failure.

In a more official context, the supreme financial authority in France, the Cour des Comptes (Languedoc-Roussillon) in 1997 denounced two associations acting as a front in Nîmes, which were subsidized by the town council. They disappeared illegally, embezzling 50 million francs (1997) and owing a similar amount to the tax department.[20]

and therefore by the taxpayers, while the rest is subsidized by the Union des Villes Taurines, so once more French taxpayers, who are blissfully unaware of this, are paying.[15]

PROFIT AND LOSS

Marc Lavie, an *aficionado* specializing in bullfight statistics, stated that in France and Spain, 'Without the *ferias*, the Las Ventas bullring would be ruinously expensive . . . a simple review of the bullfighting economy leads to one obvious fact – the bullring is virtually only full during the *ferias* nowadays'; and again: 'The spectators' financial resources are no longer able to bankroll the excessive expenditure sustained by the *fiesta* for the past fifteen years . . . the time for deflation has come.' This remarkable statistician and *aficionado* has noticed that the number of spectacles has dropped by 100 since 2003.[16] In Spain, *aficionados* claim that bullfighting supports hundreds of jobs. However, the reality is very different.[17] The bull ranches make

Despite public subsidies and support from the Ricard clubs, the Bayonne bullring, one of the largest, announced a deficit of 247,255 euros against a bullfighting budget of 2,287,976 euros (July 2008), probably without counting induced expenditure. The history of bullfighting in the small city of Fenouillet (Haute Garonne) is one of wasted public funds, well documented by activist opponents, including a young vet. According to an Ipsos poll, 81 per cent of the inhabitants of this French *département* believe that bullfighting is not part of their culture, and 62 per cent are opposed to the organization of bullfights. However, the mayor of this small town, 10 km from Toulouse, succeeded in building a temporary bullring and putting on some bullfights in 2004, which could not be prevented by an emergency interim ruling.[21] The following provides a rare insight into the way public funds are allocated to bullfighting activities:

> The city council has subsidized as Associations Law 1901: 1. 'for the promotion of bullfighting' a budget of 95,000 euros;

Bullring in Las Ventas, Madrid, home to the Circo Americano, December 2008.

Former bullring of Vista Alegre, district of Carabanchel, Madrid, now a multi-purpose auditorium.

2. *Pena Garona*, organized by the Mayor of Fenouillet; 3. *Las Morenas*, by his wife; 4. another by a rugby player. Satellite expenditure, for example: subsidy for a building that has become a restaurant, given to a chef, a friend of the mayor, with a bullfighting *bodega*; a trip for schoolchildren to Spain to introduce them to bullfighting culture; repairing the nocturnal damage after bullfights and maintenance of the temporary bullring (protective fencing, car park). The subsidies received come from: the community of Grand Toulouse: 94,000 euros; the Parliamentary Reserve Fund: 61,000 euros; the General Council: 56,000 euros; the Regional Council: 2,300 euros.

The association for the promotion of bullfighting, Tolosa Toros, financed by public funds,[22] drew up an acknowledgement of their failure and requested a subsidy for the 2006 session, having recorded a large deficit 'posing a serious threat to the economic viability of the Feria de Fenouillet' and the poor quality of a bullfight in which a bull had leaped into the *callejon* (the narrow passageway between the *barrera* and the spectators' stands) and had been killed with a sword. In Hemingway's words, there is one conclusion: 'Of all things financial that I have any acquaintance with the dirtiest in regard to money is bullfighting'.[23]

FOR AND AGAINST

A poll taken in October–November 2003 for the Franz Weber foundation concerned three non-bullfighting countries, Germany, Switzerland and Belgium, the last-named facing criticism for cockfighting, and three bullfighting countries, Portugal, France and Spain. The opponents

(ranging from 56.5 to 95.9 per cent) were in the majority everywhere, but the *afición*, who was very much in the minority, helped to fill the bullrings by travelling from one to another. Bullfighting fans were recruited from the intelligentsia (Germany, France) or from the fairly wealthy upper middle classes. In Spain, the intellectuals joined the opposition, faced with a more working-class bullfighting fan base, as was the case in Belgium, which was probably sensitized to this type of spectacle by cockfighting. In the Nîmes bullring in 2004, 10.25 per cent of the spectators were not French. The fan base seemed to have connections to French-speaking communities in Belgium and Switzerland.

Women were slightly in the majority among opponents of both sexes and slightly in the minority among *aficionados* of both sexes, except in Germany, where they were very much in the minority. The fan base followed a practically identical development in the three countries where *aficionados* were few and far between (Switzerland, Belgium, Germany). Their love of the spectacle fell off at around the age of 65. Spain was the only country where the number of *aficionados* and opponents was roughly equal:

Protesting against bullfighting.

Campaigning for a bullfighting-free Europe, Brussels, June 2008.

in the 45–55 years age bracket, those for and against were equal (around 40). A study in Italy would be informative, since that country has had experience of animal fighting and bullrings, and did ban bullfighting, refusing to allow Mussolini to stage a 'half-idiotic, half-cruel parody'.[24]

In Spain, city-dwellers' interest in bullfighting dropped from 10.4 to 7.4 per cent between 2002 and 2006; while the complete lack of interest increased from 68.9 to 72.1 per cent. A survey carried out by the Ministry of Culture throughout Spain looked at the attendance at one bullfight in 2003: 8.6 per cent of those surveyed had attended several bullfights, and 91.4 per cent had not attended any. The data by region, charted on a map, showed that continuing interest in bullfighting was, broadly speaking, found in the centre of

Spain, as opposed to Mexico, where it was located along the Pacific coast. The bullfighting public is ageing throughout the world. In Spain, according to El País on 28 December 2006, the majority of bullfighting fans are in the over-69 age group, which is similar to the situation in Nîmes, where 58 per cent of fans are in their sixties. In Spain, therefore, the bullfighting fan base is made up of survivors of Francoism. The study by age groups shows that the majority of young people in Spain, Portugal and France are opposed to bullfighting; with regard to the older sections of society, opponents are in the minority in Spain, but elsewhere they are in the vast majority.

In Mexico, the poll carried out in 1998 in nine regions estimated that the bullfighting public represented between 6 and 16 per cent of the population. Colima and Nuevo Leon with the industrial metropolis of Monterrey (16 per cent) were the most bullfighting-friendly. The trend had been reversed in Jalisco, which had turned its back on bullfighting (6 per cent) while Sonora (13 per cent) had become part of the North American *afición*.

In Peru a survey by the Opinión Pública Group (University of Lima) looked at 34 districts of the Lima-Callao Metropolis, representing 94.74 per cent of the electorate. Opposition to bullfighting, which has prevailed since 2004, continues to grow: 63.2 per cent in 2003; 72.7 per cent in 2004; 78.1 per cent in 2005; and 82 per cent in 2006. These figures show a rejection of 83.1 per cent compared with 14.4 per cent acceptance. 'Given that the population still does not know the full facts about the spectacle, it is hoped that this figure will improve.'[25] In Ecuador, bullfighting is supported by the dominant political class, owing to public funds. On average, 1,000 seats are occupied in the main bullring, which has a seating capacity of 8,000 spectators. In Colombia, bullfights are held in ten of the fifteen departments, in twelve permanent bullrings (between 3,000 and 10,000 spectators) and several temporary bullrings, during the course of some ten annual *ferias*. Bullfighting is supported by President Alvaro Uribe's brother, who is a breeder. They are broadcast on television, but although the ratings are very poor the opposition is muzzled. In Venezuela, the bullring in Caracas has been closed since the mid-1990s. Militants try to influence opinion and to persuade well-known personalities to take up their cause. The 'Groupe media' provides an umbrella for Latin-American bullfighting opponents.

Since 2000, impresarios have been trying to export bullfighting to new markets. In Israel, Rabbi Ovadia Yosef reminded people that the Torah does not tolerate animal maltreatment for the purposes of entertainment and, in the Jerusalem Press Agency, he wrote 'God does not want you to go to places where people amuse themselves with cruelty to animals' (8 August 2004). In Russia the Orthodox Church thwarted plans for bullfights. As for the Islamic world, it is believed that any cruel sport involving animals is incompatible with the Koran. In China a planned bullfight in Beijing was cancelled in 2003 due to pressure from numerous animal protection demonstrations. The bullfight of 6 October 2004, scheduled to take place at the Stadium in Shanghai, was cancelled, but then held on 23/24 October in Yangpu Stadium (province of Shanghai) with picadors, but without killing the bull, contrary to the promise of the advertisements. There have also been unsuccessful attempts to stage bullfights in Chengdu (2005) and Chongqing (2006).

A contradictory situation prevails in the bullfighting countries: in view of the public funds needed to subsidize a spectacle that is rejected by the vast majority of taxpayers, no one could begin an investigation without asking 'Who benefits from the crime?'

Mikhail Dlugach, *The Russian Bullfighter*.

Juan Belmonte before the kill. In *Death in the Afternoon*, Hemingway said the unrivalled Belmonte 'would wind a bull around him like a belt'.

eleven

The Fight against Bullfighting Today

Elias Canetti once analysed the effects of the conical layout of the bullring:

> The crowd is seated opposite itself. Every spectator has a thousand in front of him, a thousand heads . . . Their visible excitement increases his own. There is no break in the crowd which sits like this, exhibiting itself to itself . . . The tiered ring of fascinated faces has something strangely homogenous about it . . . Any gap in the ring might remind him of disintegration and subsequent dispersal. But there is no gap; this crowd is doubly closed, to the world outside and in itself.[1]

Violent death 'moves us so profoundly only because it works on the group itself, and because in one way or another it transfigures and redeems in its own eyes'.[2]

The function of the crowd is to provide justification: it is not possible that 'all these people could be wrong', an inquisitor once explained to a young woman awaiting execution.[3] The voice of the masses finds expression in the tremendous clamour that spreads through the town like the stream of blood suggested by a poster by Miguel Barceló (1988), which shows a red tide flowing from the bullring and submerging Nîmes. Everyone is affected by crowd pressure. In his *Confessions*, St Augustine considers the volte-face of an opponent who had come to the amphitheatre to prove his indifference: 'As soon as he saw the blood, he at once drank in savagery . . . He was not now the person who had come in, but just one of the crowd which he had joined . . . he took the madness home with him so that it urged him to return, not only with those by whom he had originally been drawn there, but even more than them, taking others with him'.[4]

Active opposition to blood sports and other forms of animal cruelty can on occasion involve almost as much risk as bullfighting. On 1 February 1994, for example, Jill Phipps, an animal rights campaigner and single mother, fell under the wheels of a lorry carrying calves, as she tried to block its way to Coventry airport, during a demonstration against the ill-treatment of calves for veal on the Continent. Nine years earlier Vicki Moore, filming too close to a bull being tortured in the village of Coria, found herself in the path of the animal which was crazed with terror and pain; she later died in 2000 from complications caused by her initial injuries.[5]

The manipulation of modes of expression is one device used to camouflage violence, 'as if the narrator, not being the perpetrator [of the violence] was taking care to emphasize, using a tone hostile to the crude acts he was commenting on, his own distance [from it]';[6] this is, in fact, the casual tone employed by certain television

Miguel Barceló, poster design for the Nîmes festival, 1988.

presenters. Comedy is another commonplace distancing device. The *desplante* (an oblique posture in fencing) is carried out by certain matadors by way of a challenge, for example, pretending to make a phone call between the bull's horns. Pierre Paris, who became director of the French Institute in Madrid in 1922 told how, at the Alcalá bullring (1895), he was deeply distressed by the sight of a 'walking corpse, its entrails swinging, (which) went straight past him, looking crazed, bringing tears to his eyes . . .', but he was even more horrified, the next day, by the journalist's ironic commentary: 'the bull says to the corpse: walk and the corpse walks'.[7]

Hemingway thought that the 'death of the horse tends to be comic' because the animal 'gallops in a stiff old-maidish fashion around the ring trailing the opposite of clouds of glory'.[8] In Spanish and Mexican comic bullfights, the *cuadrillas*, sometimes made up of dwarfs, kill bull calves and dance on the bloody corpses to 'amuse the children'.[9] In a lithograph of Bordeaux, Goya depicted the spectators laughing at one injured man. The artist's amusement completely divorces the executioner from his victim. A photograph of a grinning El Cordobés on his knees before a dying animal on the ground takes this shameful behaviour to its limit. 'The absence of feeling which usually accompanies laughter'[10] ensures the spectators are of like mind. The singer, Francis Cabrel, wonders, through the intermediary of the bull, about men who are capable of 'amusing themselves on a tomb'; the bull says 'I hear them laugh as I breathe my last.'[11]

A technical initiatory vocabulary generally works 'to exorcize any vague desire for pity from the bullring'.[12] There is world of difference between the mellifluous sound of the phrase *sacar la espada* and its harsh reality, as described by Jean-Paul Sartre in 1939: 'The beasts bled all they had, and it took four tries to kill them. The ineffectual sword stuck in the back of their necks was yanked out with a cane ("why not use an umbrella", said Bost furious) and another was

plunged in, and so forth, until they fell.'[13] André Franquin demystified the technical language of bullfighting in a cartoon.[14] A bull is parading proudly around the ring after killing the matador. Skewered on its horns are the victor's usual trophies, the ears and tail. Various *aficionado* spectators vie with each other to show off their expertise: 'Yes, yes, look, he's got the two ears and the tail', one says, not realising that the trophies belong to the dead matador, but then one woman remarks in Spanish: 'He has cut off both ears and the *zizi*' (*zizi* is slang for penis).

Festive props, such as the bright colours, music and television commentaries, eradicate any notion of cruelty in a spectacle that is regarded as natural. Violence, when unidentified, is invisible.[15]

Francisco Goya, 'Another madness of his [Martincho] in the Same Ring [Saragossa]', from *Tauromaquia*, 1816, etching.

Carlo Aires, *Untitled*, 'Happily ever after' series, double *torero* dwarf in the Los Bombero company in Madrid, 2007.

Violence, once it has been passively accepted and then trivialized, stops being personal and becomes axiomatic (accepted without proof). Violence is legalized, initially locally, becoming indispensable to the overall structure, then spreads to large cities, then states, creating a precedent that gives rise to other laws, like the Spanish law of 1918 banning the humanitarian slaughter of animals in favour of the *puntilla* (dagger) used in bullfighting.

The relatively recent science of victimology initially identifies the direct, active physical attacks on the bull, including the acts of maltreatment behind the scenes, like shaving the horns, which occurs so frequently that there is a fixed price for the service.[16] It should also be remembered that, when added together, the injuries inflicted on the bull from the various weapons would total about 1.50 metres – approximately the animal's height at its withers. Indirect, less instantaneous maltreatments include the exhausting cape passes, purgatives, salt to make the animal thirsty, an array of drugs, overheating in the sun, the restrictive dimensions of the crates with sloping floors used for transport and the length of the journey; Pierre Molas, a qualified professional bullfight promoter, declared that on one occasion 'the two official vets, who attended the loading as required by law, pretended to see nothing, in accordance with that unwritten law, the law of silence, which is much more readily obeyed than the former.' Verbal attacks, which are not as easy to pinpoint, include calling for the bull: although a kindly act in the fields, this becomes a provocative ruse to make the animal charge in the bullring. Mental cruelty include the separation of the bull from its herd, its necessary social environment, as well as its obvious fear. The bull displays other, subtler, signs of distress, like the direction of its ears or the revulsion in its eyes, so accurately observed by Goya. 'Specific neurological or endocrine clues are commonly used by biologists and veterinarians, while facial expressions, body language and behaviour are used by ethologists.'[17]

Several practising matadors, some of them 'reformed', say that they have seen bulls with tears in their eyes, although it is unclear whether this is a simple discharge or an expression of emotion. Finally, verbal attacks can also include successively transforming the bull into a superman or a sub-animal, into a god or meat, thereby denying its animality and, ultimately, its capacity for suffering. The bull is literally 'denatured' by the breeder, who introduces aggression to its makeup. Forced to enter the bullring, the bull has a place in the science and law of victimology because, unlike the matador, the animal has not chosen to entertain the spectators at the expense of its own suffering.

TURNING CHILDREN INTO KILLERS

'Five-year-old children, armed with small clubs, shouting, whacking stones in the street . . . donkeys, chickens, people, like a huge herd of bulls': this was the sight seen by villagers on their way to a bullfighting festival.[18] The media spotlight is currently on 'young . . . Michelito, who confronts good-sized bull calves, and has killed around 60 since the age of six. This has encouraged fans of bullfighting to suggest bringing Michelito to France'.[19] In France, a ban on allowing children in the bullring has come up against commercial and ideological proselytism, in addition to opposition from certain Deputies, who put their passion for bullfighting before their duty. However 'at a time when people are concerned about the rising violence of which young people can be either the perpetrators, witnesses or victims, it is vital to ban access to bullfights for minors under sixteen, even when accompanied by an adult', retorted an influential member of the Green Party, in agreement with most psychiatrists, who emphasize the perversity of allowing children to become accustomed to a violence that is sanctioned by adults.[20] The philosopher Elisabeth de Fontenay insists that this practice is unacceptable.[21] French bullfighting schools are subsidized by the town councils (Arles, Nîmes and South-West France) and even, in Tarascon, by the French Child Benefit Office. From nursery school age, children attending these schools are taken by the coachload to studios where they draw blood-covered bulls; from the age of eight they handle weapons, then wash the blood from the bullring, before illegally killing bull calves at private ranches. Pablo Knudsen's ten hours of footage bears witness to the triple horror of exultant children, tortured animals and adults applauding the carnage.

Christina García Rodero's photograph of children gathered around the bloodied head of a bull freshly slaughtered.

Children made excellent hired killers (*sicarii*) during the *Violencia* in Medellín; in Naples they were hired at the age of twelve by the Mafia; they serve as soldiers during current genocides in Africa. Various 'Mozarts of the bullfighting world' were incredibly decisive in their killing. Pepito Bienvenida succeeded in executing a classic *volapié*, which was confirmed by the autopsy carried out on his bull: out of 27 autopsies performed on fighting bulls, the only *estocada* that hit the heart was executed by the twelve-year-old matador.[22] However, El Juli, who killed publically on the day of his first communion, did not win unanimous support from the bullfighting public, who criticized his 'perverted innocence'. Hemingway wrote: 'natural ability and early training, commencing the training with calves where there is no danger, have made bullfighters

Arman, poster design for the *Feria de Nîmes*, 1995.

of men with no natural courage'.[23] José Arroyo Delgado 'tried to forget an unhappy childhood . . . by dealing the death blow (at the age of eleven) to his first calf on 7 June 1981';[24] Almodóvar's *Matador* felt that 'to stop killing is to stop living'. Children's bullfights (or *becerrades*), banned in Spain, are authorized in Mexico, where there are appearances by *cuadrillas* of children.[25] The spectators at bullfights performed every summer by young teenagers include children, sometimes aged three or four, who admire their big brothers 'dressed in their suits of light'. They are taught to euphemize or deny the cruelty, which weakens their moral sense. This creates confusion, particularly since the act of noticing pain in others activates neurological mechanisms that are partially shared by the mental process that allows witnesses to feel pain themselves.[26] The keen

Teenage apprentice matador in Pablo Knudsen's
Apprendre à tuer, 2007.

natural empathy children feel for animals height-
ens this phenomenon. 'So it is not harmless to
show children a spectacle in which an animal is
being tortured publically for entertainment. It is
even utterly irresponsible.'[27]

DOGMAS

In half a century, the Catholic Church's clergy
have never objected to the cruelty of bullfighting,
nor have its ecclesiastical supporters. Although
Pope John Paul II never granted an interview to
the anti-bullfighting campaigners recommended
by a French bishop, he met with several matadors.
The Vatican has never responded to the international petitions with millions of signatures. The
counsellor at the French embassy, Monseigneur
Yves Gouyou, shows off his passion for bullfighting in his living-room, which is filled with
souvenirs from bullfights. The official Catechism
of the Catholic Church strikes a false balance:
one paragraph advocates respect for Creation, but
the following paragraph gives man dominion over
animals, including for use in entertainment.[28]
However, the Papal Bull issued by Pius V remains

canonically legal, and all the other monotheistic
religions have condemned bullfighting. But several
voices are making themselves heard: Monseigneur
Roland Minnerath wrote and published in his
diocesan bulletin: 'In the name of respect and
of life . . . a human being cannot take pleasure
in violence towards animals.'[29] Other prelates
are expressing similar opinions.

Various renowned theologians are sensitive
to the plight of animals and their defenders. Eugen
Drewermann, a German, and Revd Andrew
Linzey, an Englishman, are little known in France.
The latter has founded a Centre in Oxford to
bring together international thinkers concerned
with animal rights. Linzey recalls that the Anglican
Church was involved in the first animal protection association in 1824. In his view, the Humanitarian Theory entails respect for all living, feeling
creatures, and is opposed to Thomism, which es-
chews the notion of kindness to God's creatures.

Animals have 'theos-rights' (literally 'God-
rights') because it is the right of God which
establishes the specific value of some living
beings. In this sense, rights are not awarded,
accorded or bestowed but recognized. When
we speak of animal rights we conceptualize
what is objectively owed to animals as a
matter of justice by virtue of their Creator's
right.[30]

The five reasons listed by Linzey for rejecting
bullfighting,[31] include this one: 'wantonness
indicates . . . a moral meanness of life . . . To act
wantonly to animals is to deny their moral status
. . . wantonness violates God's right in Creation'.
On bullfighting, Linzey wrote: 'To breed and rear
creatures for gratuitous destruction is not simply
human perversity but a reversal of divine purpose'.

Among other Protestants, Pastor Simon Sire-Fougères published *Mortelle Corrida* in Beziers:

> By feeding Cain, who is fascinated by violence and thirsty for blood, do we not keep alive the deadly bullfight that involves the murder of brother by brother, a human tragedy that history repeats time and time again? Didn't the Prophet Isaiah, bewailing the sins of Judah, declare 'I delight not in the blood of bullocks, or of lambs, or of he-goats'?[32]

Since 1950, scientific discoveries have proved that human beings and animals share many similarities. The discovery of DNA and subsequent developments in molecular genetics confirm, among other things, the shared origin of all life. Animal ethology (behavioural science) has shown that animal culture is transmissible like human cultural behaviour, and that certain tools attributed to prehistoric man are actually the work of monkeys.

These discoveries condemn all extreme anthropocentrism. Jacques Derrida, committed 'to seeing the world, life . . . quite differently, beyond all divisions, all the borders that divide and separate', stressed the cruel nature of the relationship between mankind and animals: 'This subjection, whose history we are trying to interpret, can be called violence. Men do everything they can to conceal this cruelty or hide it from themselves so that this violence, that some might compare to the worst genocides, can be disregarded or minimized'. During his final years, the French philosopher became involved with the Comité Radicalement Anti-Corrida (CRAC, Alès), which benefited from his renown.[33] Many other philosophers, thinkers or writers have tackled and denounced 'this heritage, which has become so shameful',[34] or, along with

Graffiti on the Badajoz road (Extremadura): 'Would you torture your dog? (Bulls neither)'.

the Spanish philosopher Jesús Mosterín, have rejected 'torture as entertainment'.[35] Among the most widely translated authors, Peter Singer (1975) or Tom Reagan (1983) have developed some seminal thoughts on animal exploitation. In the past half-century or so, many internationally known figures have joined the opposition to bullfighting, ranging from the writer Jack Kerouac, Yannick Noah, the Olympic tennis champion, Alain Delon, the long-famous actor, Almodóvar's favourite actress, Rossy de Palma, and the Spanish singer Alaska, who posed naked with three *banderillas* stuck in her back. Madonna cultivated the paradox, which was no doubt profitable, of supposedly being a vegetarian and shooting videos of bullfights.[36]

OPPOSING VIOLENCE

The rejection of radical anthropocentrism represented a genuine revolution that could be called Copernican – characterized by a slow start, but giving rise to a new generation of younger, more numerous animal protectors, the majority of whom are now men. Starting in the 1960s, various specialist associations have been founded to protect cattle: in France, an association was founded to protect farm animals slaughtered for food (Jacqueline Gilardoni, 1964); in England, Peter and Anna Roberts set up Compassion in World Farming to monitor breeding and intensive breeding (1967); and in France, around 1990, the PMAF was set up to protect farm animals. In Spain, the anti-bullfighting campaign was revived in 1960 by Wenceslao Fernandez Florez, in France in the following decade by Andrée Valadier and also by Alfred Kastler, first President of the French League for Animal Rights. The Universal Declaration of Animal Rights was proclaimed at the UNESCO headquarters in 1978.

An injured horse in the bullring, Jérôme.

In 1984, faced with the growing number of illegal bullfights and the promotion of the Nîmes bullring, the Comité Radicalement Anti-Corrida (CRAC, Alès) was founded. From 1990 onwards, the French animal rights campaigner François Cavanna revived anti-bullfighting criticism. In complete contrast to the sophistry of some contemporary writing, his deliberately crude language demystified the orgasmic experience: 'Supreme thrill . . . which on the terraces . . . dampens old ladies' panties and makes impotent men semi-hard.'[37] In 1993 the journalist Luce Lapin began writing pieces condemning the maltreatment of animals, followed by a regular column in *Charlie Hebdo*. The *Puces de Luce Lapin* soon became popular and *Charlie Hebdo* was the only French newspaper for many years that regularly denounced the maltreatment of animals. In 2005 Jérôme Lescure declared that 'I dedicated my film [*Alinéa 3*] . . . to that brown bull whose eyes looked straight into my camera'. Luce Lapin added: 'the images . . . haunt me . . . The suffering and death of a living creature, human or animal, cannot be trivialized in any way'.[38]

In 1986 in Madrid a group of four people initiated some awareness-raising activities and demonstrations supported by ecologists, then organized the first international anti-bullfighting demonstration in 1988, bringing together eleven European countries. George Roos, the South American poet and writer, and Vicki Moore supported this group, with ADDA (Asociación Defensa Derechos Animal) in Catalonia. By the end of the twentieth century, anti-bullfighting activity could be found everywhere. In Latin America in Mexico City, led by Emma de Saldaña, in France in Beziers, supported by Théodore Monod (COLBAC).

Today, all the bullfighting countries now have anti-bullfighting associations. The internet deprived bullfighting fans and journalists of their monopoly on information and enabled the opposition to benefit from internationalization. At the end of the twentieth century the largest non-specialized animal protection associations joined forces with anti-bullfighting campaigners, for example the English WSPA (World Society for the Protection of Animals).

The present situation can be traced back via the following key events. In 1979 the Swiss Franz Weber Foundation created an International Court of Justice for Animal Rights. Three sessions were devoted to bullfighting in Spain (1982, 2003, 2008). In 2008, the Portuguese plaintiffs accused the President of the Republic, Jorge Sampaio, of introducing Spanish bullfighting into Portugal, where this spectacle is banned by law and overwhelmingly rejected by the people. Various large associations organized international demonstrations. People for the Ethical Treatment of Animals (PETA) organized a parade of scantily clad activists in Pamplona, which has become a

Anti-bullfighting demonstration, Pamplona, July 2006.

popular international event for young protestors. Since 2002 the demonstration by Anima Naturalis (Pamplona, 5 July 2008) has obtained press coverage extending over five newspapers in Latin America, Italy (*Republica*) and Germany (*Focus*) as well as in *Think Spain*. Protestors demonstrated in front of the famous Guggenheim Museum in Bilbao with *banderillas* in their backs (Equanimal, 2008). These examples are enough to show an inventive approach that now receives a great deal of media coverage.

On an international scale, these campaigns include the victorious fight of the industrialist Steve Hindi against the soft-drink giant Pepsi-Cola, a bullfighting sponsor. A film linking Pepsi-Cola advertising to gory scenes from bullfights was shown throughout America from the 'Slam Van'.[39] Other associations, followed by the animal rights activist Maneka Gandhi, threatened to boycott Pepsi. Wrongfully denounced as a terrorist and arrested by FBI experts, Steve Hindi was proved innocent and Pepsi withdrew its sponsorship of bullrings.

The Dutch Comité Anti Stierenvechten (CAS International) was founded in 1990 with the World Society for the Protection of Animals (WSPA), after a request from the Spanish animal protection society (ADDA). Its aim is to put a stop to so-called 'artistic events' using animals. Run by professionals, the CAS attacks the promotion of bullfighting outside Spain, often successfully. This association acts peacefully, informs the public about the cruelty of bullfights, lobbies the European institutions and governments concerned and provides financial aid to militants in bullfighting countries.

The first International Summit of ANTI-CORRIDA was organized in Lisbon in May 2007 sponsored by Tyto Alba, with the ANIMAL association (Lisbon) and the CAS. The international demonstration in front of the Pequeno Campo bullring in Lisbon made a considerable public impact. Sponsorship of the Second International Summit in Brussels in 2008 enabled the CAS to work in conjunction with European Members of Parliament to found an organization 'for a bullfighting-free Europe', faced with an exhibition by the pro-bullfight lobby at the European Parliament, which was subsidized by public funds, particularly Spanish and French. European publications provided documented replies to the arguments of the *afición*.

Apart from bullfighting countries, several organizations criticized tour operators selling tickets for bullfights or the cruel Spanish *fiestas* (Tick Tack Ticket). 'We find it incomprehensible that a company as well respected as British Airways would wish to blatantly publicize such a savage spectacle as the *Toro de la Vega* (13 September 2007, Irish Council against Blood Sports). Members of the public could wager on the number of trophies, the bull's ears and tail, that might be awarded to a particular matador. A commercial shot by Pablo Knudsen shows these body parts being removed from the living bull (ICAB). In Lisbon the state-owned channel RTP (Radio Television Portugal) withdrew bullfighting programmes as a result of lobbying by ANIMAL (18 July 2008), which went on to attack the Vila Galé Hotels Group, which owned a fighting bull ranch (September, 2008). One of the anti-bullfighting tour operators, the Canadian Mac-Donald Tours informed *aficionados* 'Although you may attract one client, you will put off ten others'; it threatened to boycott the French bullfighting towns. In France, the famous Routard guide wrote fearlessly: 'We have already advised against the zoos . . . the same goes for bullfights . . .'.[40]

Imaginative bullfighting opponents invented alternative solutions, for example: an association in Valencia (Venezuela, 1 August 2007) offered spectators an alternative to the bullfight in the form of a free concert at the entrance to the bull-ring by renowned orchestras, with the slogan *Musica o Muerte*.

The classic street demonstration assumed a variety of new forms: slogans on placards read: 'Silence, torture in progress' and spectators had to pass a guard of dishonour, called the corridors of shame (FLAC). Simple balloons filled with hydrogen outside the Madrid bullring in the late 1980s succeeded in carrying a protest placard into the bullring with the help of the wind. At the bullring in Beziers in 1995, seven men hoisted the word 'Torture' on placards. In the bullring at Alès, demonstrators chained themselves together in the bullring. Giant poster displays became the norm: in Nice, on the Promenade des Anglais, in front of the Negresco hotel, which supported bullfighting; 12-metre-square signs in the Paris Metro, initiated by Albert Jacquard, proclaimed *Corrida la Honte* (Bullfighting is a Disgrace). Stylish new anti-bullfighting pamphlets designed by the ASAC (Alliance Contre La Corrida) were handed out at the Avignon Theatre Festival, and in 2007 an aeroplane flew over the bullring in Nîmes towing an anti-bullfighting banner.

In May 2008 Spanish militants (Igualdad Animal), quite the opposite of *espontaneos* (amateurs who jump into the ring to cape the bull illegally), jumped into the Madrid bullring in the middle of a San Isidro bullfight, brandishing placards; hardened climbers unfurled a vertical banner from the dizzy heights of the Las Ventas bullring, proclaiming *Prohibición!* Other similar events were organized in Barcelona. Films about anti-bullfighting achievements were so successful

at mobilizing adolescents that the journal *Toros* acknowledged a 'bombardment by the enemies of bullfighting that grows stronger with each passing day'.[41] The journalists exploited these events, putting an end to the silence. In 2007, only a handful of backward contributors at the *Figaro* were continuing to defend bullfighting.

Various cartoonists put their talents at the disposal of the anti-bullfighting lobby; although these individuals were formerly mavericks and often amateurs, there are now a vast number of professionals in the field. The dramatic drawings by Cabu or Tignous express with savage energy the indignation felt by any normal person in the face of torture, whether of animals or human beings. Various talented letter-writers tirelessly lambast the politicians. The Dutch academic Michèle Breut has been sending classic epistles to politicians for years: 'The sadistic torturers, the pro-bullfighting literature and the media, which are their accomplices, are counterfeiters.' Quoting Gide, she concluded: 'in a world where everyone cheats, it's the true man who looks like a charlatan.'

Before 1990 several towns, one of the first being Tossa del Mar in Spain, declared that they were closed to bullfighting. There are about 50 towns now, mainly in Catalonia, plus three in France (Mouans-Sartoux), which are officially anti-bullfighting towns. In Barcelona the abolition of bullfighting came up against organized opposition. The town's sumptuous bullring of 1914–16, seating 20,000, was managed by the Balaña group, then promoted by 72 appearances by Manolete. Interest waned despite a performance by José Tomás in 2000. An animal protection law of 2003 obtained by the Convergencia i Unio nationalists banned bullrings that could be dismantled, and admission to children under fourteen.[42] In

Pedro Balaña, 'Empresario Modelo', in the 1940s.

Catalonia, bullfighting has become an old-fashioned, right-wing event. According to a survey published by the Spanish Ministry of Culture, 98.2 per cent of Catalonians did not attend a bullfight in 2003. The bullring was losing 24,000 euros per *feria*. The 5,000 square metres of the arena were highly coveted; Jordi Portabella, second deputy mayor of Barcelona, attempted to negotiate with the Balaña group. 'If Catalonia manages to abolish bullfighting, it would appear to be a sophisticated nation dragging the rest of Spain towards modernity'.[43] In Spain, animals entered the political arena. The Partido Antitaurino came eighth in Catalonia (with 13,730 votes). The prospective abolition of bullfighting by the Catalan Parliament had to be ratified in Madrid.

Various prestigious towns in Latin America have also become anti-bullfighting. In January 2007 the mayor of Zapatosa (Colombia), Octavio Gutiérrez Rueda, dedicated the town's bullring to festivals that 'celebrate life', after the last bullfight of 2007. The town council of Medellin (Colombia, 16 February 2008) respected the desire of the popular majority (92 per cent of voters) to reject cruel entertainments like circuses or bullfighting. In France, the Deputy for Les Alpes-Maritimes showed great courage, in a government that was almost officially protecting bullfighting, by filing an application for a modification (8 June 2004) to Article 521-1 of the French Penal Code (then Alinéa 3), which abolished the legal exception in favour of bullfighting. In order to gain access to accounts showing the subsidies granted to bullfighting by their neighbouring mayor's office, which had refused to cooperate, the militants had to go through a Parisian organization; the procedure lasted two years (Commission d'Accès aux Documents Administratifs, CADA).

The Green Parties were the first in the world to include animals in their manifesto, an example followed belatedly in France. The Mexican Green Party, with 126 Deputies and 3 Senators (1998), was supported by the English branch of the WSPA against bullfighting and pro respect for life.[44] In the presidential elections in France, Dominic Voynet's manifesto was the only one to condemn bullfighting. Current government responses claim to believe that 50 per cent of French citizens belong to the *afición*. In Spain, the Anti-Bullfighting Party Against Animal Maltreatment (PACMA) was the revelation of March 2008; after becoming the fourteenth strongest political force in the country, its 200,000 votes allowed it to overtake various well-known parties.[45] Anti-bullfighting

Sabine Joosten, *Bull in a Field*, photograph.

associations on both continents regularly file requests to the political authorities for legal protection for animals (for example, Ecuador). ASOGUAU (Venezuela) is keen to abolish *toros coleados*, prevent children from entering bullrings and close the bullring in Valencia. Anima Naturalis (May 2008, Luis Tascon, Deputy) filed for legal protection (Caracas). In September 2008 the ANIMAL association in Lisbon, which is very militant in legal matters, successfully campaigned to have a rodeo abolished by the Court of Justice in Faro (Algarve, a popular tourist region), which acknowledged its cruelty.

In most bullfighting countries, the gap seems to be widening between increasingly well-informed public opinion and the disinformation disseminated through images on the television. An episode that took place in France is typical: the Bureau de Vérification de la Publicité (BVP) is formed of self-appointed advertising professionals who monitor television advertising and provide generally effective opposition. A commercial by the Société

Protectrice des Animaux denouncing the cruelty of bullfighting and narrated by the French singer Renaud was rejected, even in the most abstract versions, which meant that the fiction was being banned rather than the reality. However, this was down to the desire to protect the commercial interests of the bullfighting world. The report, shown on the television news, was enough to demonstrate the mercenary nature of this so-called monitoring.

References

one: Fighting Bulls

1 Claude Martel, 'Le Vocabulaire des gens de bovine, l'Espagnol de la corrida', in *L'Homme et le taureau*, ed. Jean-Noël Pelen and Claude Martel (Grenoble, 1990), p. 120.

2 Suzanne Antoine, 'La Protection pénale de l'animal domestique', *Le Droit de l'animal* (Paris, 2007), pp. 69–70.

3 Hannah Velten, *Cow* (London, 2007), p. 73.

4 Margarita Torrione, *Cronica festiva de dos reinados en la Gaceta de Madrid, 1700–1759* (Malaga, 1998), *Gaceta*, 6, Madrid, 1 February 1707, p. 60.

5 Serge Grunzinski, *L'Amérique de la conquête* (Paris, 1991), p. 174.

6 Fabio Martinez, *El viajero y la memoria* (Universidad Pontificia Bolivariana, 2000), p. 63.

7 Bernard Fouques, 'L'Indien d'Amérique latine ou le part maudite' in *L'Histoire inhumaine*, ed. Guy Richard (Paris, 1992), pp. 365–411.

8 Keith Thomas, *Man and the Natural World* (London, 1983), pp. 183–4.

9 Timothy Mitchell, *Blood Sport: A Social History of Spanish Bullfighting* (Philadelphia, 1991), pp. 16–21.

10 José Vargas Ponce, *Dissertacion sobre la corrida de toros compuesta en 1807* (Madrid, 1961), pp. 68–70.

11 José Manuel Matilla and José Miguel Medrano, *El Libro de la Tauromaquia, Francisco de Goya* (Madrid, 2001).

12 Camille Pradier-Fodéré, *Lima et ses environs* (Paris, 1897), pp. 279–83.

13 Don Gaspar de Jovellanos, *Bread and Bulls, An apologetical oration, on the flourishing state of Spain, in the reign of King Charles IV* (1813), p. 92.

14 Anon., *Spanien wie es gegenwartig ist . . .* (Gotha, 1797), p. 213.

15 Jovellanos, *Bread and Bulls*, pp. 91–3.

16 Johann Jacob Volkmann, *Neueste Reisen durch Spanien* (Leipzig, 1785), p. 337.

17 Ernest Hemingway, *Death in the Afternoon* (London, 2000), p. 20.

18 José Delgado, alias Pepe-Hillo, *La Tauromaquia, Arte de torear* (Madrid, 1796).

19 Emmanuel Witz, *Combats de toros en Espagne*, trans. Diego Morales (Madrid, 1993).

20 *Encyclopédie ou Dictionnaire raisonné des sciences et des métiers* (Geneva, 1779), vol. XXXIII, p. 737.

21 Jean-Baptiste Senac, *Traité de la structure du coeur* (Paris, 1749), vol. II, p. 233.

22 Jean-Marcel Moriceau, *Histoire et géographie de l'élevage français* (Paris, 2005).

23 Vicente Blasco Ibanez, *Blood and Sand*, trans. W. A. Gillespie (London, 1961), p. 308.

24 Hemingway, *Death in the Afternoon*, p. 81.

25 Rafael Cabrera Bonet and Maria Artisas, *Los Toros en la pressa madrilena* (Madrid, 1991), pp. 206–23.

26 Congreso nacional de Buiatría, 1995, Faculty of veterinary medicine, National Autonomous University of Mexico, 'Report by Professors F. Santiesteban, and Aja-Guardiola' in Emma D. de Saldaña, *Las Voces del Silencio* (Mexico, 2004), pp.112–14.

27 Saldaña, *Las Voces*, p 112.

28 Pablo Knudsen, *Apprendre à tuer* (Lyon, 2007).

29 Manuel Landaeta Rosales, *La Corrida en Caracas* (Caracas, 1971).

30 Miguel de Cervantes, *The Deceitful Marriage and the Dialogue of the Dogs*, trans. William Rowlandson (London, 1970).

31 Velten, *Cow*, pp. 56–7.

32 Christian August Fischer, *Travels in Spain in 1797 and 1798* (London, 1802), pp. 82–3.

33 Théophile Gautier, *Wanderings in Spain* (London, 1853), p. 69.

34 Auguste Lafront, *La Fête espagnole des taureaux, vue par les voyageurs étrangers (XVI–XVIIIe siècles)* (Paris, 1988), p. 183.

35 Pierre Matté, *Blessures et mort du taureau de combat, étude anatomico-pathologique* (Nîmes, 1929), pp. 83–4.

36 Jean Savary des Bruslons, *Dictionnaire Universel de Commerce* (Paris, 1741), articles Anneau, Batte, Brocher.

37 Thomas Gräfe, *Vergleich des Tierschutzgesetzgebung in der Bundesrepublik Deutschland und in Spanien unter besonderer Berücksichtigung des historischen Entwicklung und der gegenwärtigen Bedeutung des Stierkampfes* (Kiel, 1997), Royal decree of 18 December 1987, §4 a (1), instructions for the slaughter of animals for food in abattoirs, p. 53.

38 R. Manuel Tovar Morato, 'Tobalo', *Barrera Sol*, no. 34 (April 1991), pp. 56–7.

39 Geneviève Fontdevoille, *Cent ans de Plumaçon* (Aire-sur-Adour, 1989), in Éric Baratay and Elisabeth Hardouin-Fugier, *La Corrida* (Paris, 1995), pp. 88–90.

40 Rafael Cabrera Bonet and Maria Artigas, *Los Toros en la pressa madrilena del siglo XVIIIe* (Madrid, 1991), p. 210.

41 Ibid., pp. 166–223.

42 Ibid., p. 166.

43 Adrian Shubert, *Death and Money in the Afternoon* (Oxford, 1999), graph. 4, p. 220, graph. 5, p. 221.

two: Capital Punishment

1 Antonio Rodriguez Villa, *La Corte Monarquia de Espana en los anos de 1636 y 1637* (Madrid, 1886), pp. 275–6.

2 Angel Lopez Cantos, *Juegos, fiestas y diversiones en l'América espanole* (Madrid, 1992), p. 170.

3 Francisco de Isla, *Descripcion de la máscara* (Madrid, 1787), p. 188, in Adrian Shubert, *Death and Money in the Afternoon* (Oxford, 1999), note 33, p. 7.

4 Jean-François Bourgoing, *Modern State of Spain* (London, 1808), vol. II, pp. 359–60.

5 Georges Clémenceau, *Le Grand Pan* (Paris, 1896), p. 354.

6 Vicente Blasco Ibanez, *Blood and Sand*, trans. W. A. Gillespie (London, 1961).

7 Ernest Hemingway, *Death in the Afternoon*

(London, 2000), p. 87.

8 Hemingway, *Death in the Afternoon*, pp. 179–80.

9 R. Schneider, 'Rites de mort à Toulouse' in *L'Exécution capitale*, ed. Régis Bertrand (Aix-en-Provence, 2003), pp. 130–50.

10 Pieter Spierenburg, *The Spectacle of Suffering* (Cambridge, 1984), p. 82.

11 Clémenceau, *Le Grand Pan*, pp. 353–5.

12 L. Puppi, *Les Supplices dans l'art, cérémonial des exécutions capitales* (Paris, 1990).

13 Jean-Marie Magnan, 'Eros tauromachique' in *La Tauromachie*, ed. R. Bérard (Paris, 2003), p. 470.

14 Jean-Marie Magnan, Lucien Clergue, *Une Faena de Curro Romero* (Paris, 1992), pp. 107, 109.

15 Wolfgang Sofsky, *Traité de la violence (Treatise on Violence)* (Paris, 1998), p. 180.

16 Elias Canetti, *Crowds and Power*, trans. Carol Stewart (London, 2000).

17 Shubert, *Death and Money*, p. 152; José Vargas Ponce, *Dissertacion sobre las corridas de toros* (Madrid, 1962), pp. 142–5, 289–95.

18 Manuel Ovilo y Otero, *Vida politica de D. Manuel Godoy, Principe de la Paz* (Madrid, 1845), pp. 96–7.

19 Jean Baudrillard, *Symbolic Exchange and Death*, trans. Iain Hamilton Grant (London, 1993), p. 167.

three: Plazas and Bullrings

1 Antonio Rodriguez Villa, *La Corte Monarquia de Espana* (Madrid, 1886), p. 297.

2 Daniela Reichert, *Plaza mayor und Plaza de Toros, architektonische Rahmen der Stierkämpfe in XVII und XVIII Jahrhundert* (Munich, 1979), pp. 105–40.

3 Marquis de Condamine, *Relation abrégée d'une voyage fait dans l'intérieur de l'Amérique méridional* (Paris, 1745).

4 M. Lessard, *Colombie, Guide Ulysse* (Montreal, 1998).

5 P. Rodriguez, 'La fiesta de toros en Colombia, siglos XVI–XIX', in *Des Toros et des hommes*, ed. A. Molinié (Paris, 1999), p. 17.

6 José Emilio Calmell, *Relato historica de la plaza de toros de Lima* (Lima, 1946).

7 Luis de Tabique, *Guia de America taurina* (Mexico, 1955).

8 Yves Hébrard, *Le Vénézuela indépendant* (Paris, 1996), p. 27.

9 Camilo José Cela, *L'aficionado* (Paris, 1992), p. 4.

10 Manuel Vicent Colita, *Piel de toro* (Barcelona, 2005), last plate (unnumbered page).

11 FAADA, *Contra argumentos a las afirmaciones de l'Industria Taurina en referencia al medio ambiente* (Barcelona, 2008), www.faada.org, n.p.

12 Benito Arias Montano (1525–1598), 'Treatise' in *Toros y bueyes, La tradicion ganadera y taurina de la dehesa* (Badajoz, 2008), Fabiano Andrés Oyola, p. 23.

13 José Delgado, alias Pepe-Hillo, *La Tauromaquia, Arte de torear* (Madrid, 1796); trans. F. Paris (Sables, 2000).

14 François Coréal, *Voyages de François de Coreal aux Indes occidentales* (Amsterdam, 1722), vol. I, p. 129.

15 Oyola, *Toros*, pp. 64–7.

16 Bartolomé Bennassar, *Histoire de la Tauromachie* (Paris, 2002), p. 42.

17 Faada, *Contra* (n.p.)

18 Adrian Shubert, *Death and Money in the Afternoon* (Oxford, 1999), p. 219, graph 2.f.

19 Tudela de l'Orden, *Historia de la ganaderia Hispano Americana* (Madrid, 1993) p. 180 etc.

20 Francisco Lopez-Izquierdo, *Los Toros del nuevo mundo* (Madrid, 1992), p. 80.

21 Antonio Garcia-Baquero Gonzalez, *La Carrera de Indias* (Paris, 1997).

22 Jacques Soustelle 'Une danse dramatique mexicaine, "Le torito"', *Journal des Américanistes* (1941), pp. 155–64.

23 Ernest Hemingway, *Death in the Afternoon* (London, 2000), p. 109.

24 Francis de Castelnau, *Expédition dans les parties centrales de l'Amérique du sud, 1843–47* (Paris, 1851), vol. IV.

25 John Lloyd Stephens, *Incidents of Travel in Central America, Chiapas and Yucatan (1822)* (London, 1854), p. 184.

26 Désiré Charnay, *Voyage au Mexique, 1858–1861* (Paris, 2001), p. 88.

27 Henri de Saussure, *Voyage aux Antilles et au Mexique, 1854–56* (Geneva, 1993), p. 97.

28 Lopez-Izquierdo, *Los Toros*, p. 47.

29 John Steuert, *Narracion de una expedicion a la capital de la nueva Grenada y residencia alli de once menses, 1836–7*, pp. 114–15, in *Bogotá en los viajeros extranjeros del siglo XIX*, ed. Mario German Romero (Bogotá, 1989), p. 118.

30 Bullock, *Six Months' Residence and Travels in Mexico* (London, 1824).

31 Cané, *Notas de viaje*, in *Viajes por los Andes Colombianos* (Bogotá, 1976), p. 182.

32 Paul Marcoy, *Voyage à travers l'Amérique du sud, de l'Océan Pacifique à l'Océan Atlantique* (Paris, 1869), p. 298.

33 Isidore Löwenstern, *La Mexique, souvenirs d'un voyageur* (Paris, 1844), pp. 168–77.

34 Armando de Maria y Campos, *Imagen del mexicano en los toros* (Mexico, 1953), p. 185.

35 Pierre Dupuy, 'Les élevages mexicains', *Toros* (25 November 1997).

36 Pierre Chaunu, *Séville et l'Atlantique* (Paris, 1959), vol. VIII, p. 530.

37 Maria Dolorès Falacios Lopez, *Arte y toros estampa e ilustración taurina* (Madrid, 2004).

38 *Pintura poética en octavas rimas de las doce suertes o lances mal principales que aparecen en una corrida de toros*.

39 Falacios Lopez, *Arte*, p. 81.

four: What Travellers Saw

1 Pierre Bouguer and Charles Marie de la Condamine, *Relation abrégée d'un voyage fait dans l'intérieur de l'Amérique méridionale* (Paris, 1745).

2 Charles Stuart Cochrane, *Journal of a Residence and Travels in Colombia, During the Years 1823 and 1824* (London, 1825).

3 S. V. Rose, 'Tauromaquia y sociedad en el Peru virreinal', in *Des Toros et des hommes*, ed. A Molinié (Paris, 1999), pp. 151–63.

4 Alexander von Humboldt, *Voyages dans l'Amérique équinoxiale* (Paris, 1985), p. 173.

5 Danielle Demelas and Yves Saint-Geoir, *La Vie quotidienne en Amérique du sud au temps de Bolivar* (Paris, 1987), p. 133.

6 Luis de Tabique, *Guia de America taurina* (Mexico, 1955), p. 168.

7 John Lloyd Stephens, *Incidents of Travel in Central America, Chiapas and Yucatan* (London, 1854), pp. 125–6.

8 Max Radiguet, *Souvenirs de l'Amérique espagnole* (Lima, 1856).

9 William Bullock, *Six Months' Residence and Travels in Mexico* (London, 1824).

10 John Steuert, *Narracion de una expedicion a la capital de la Nueva Grenada y residencia alli de once menses, 1836–7*, in *Bogotá en los viajeros extranjeros del siglo XIX*, ed. Mario German

Romero (Bogotá, 1989), pp. 114–18.

11 Estella Erausqui, 'Aspect méconnu du Buenos Aires d'antan', in *Des Taureaux et des hommes*, ed. A. Molinié (Paris, 1999), p. 175.

12 Armando de Maria y Campos, *Imagen del mexicano en los toros* (Mexico, 1953), p. 155.

13 Paul Marcoy, *Voyage à travers l'Amérique du sud, de l'Océan Pacifique à l'Océan Atlantique* (Paris, 1869), p. 298.

14 Ernst Röthlisberger, *Viajeros por Colombia, 1885* (Bogotá, 1929), p. 129.

15 Franz Buchner, *Reise-Skissen aus Columbien und Venezuela* (Munich, 1888), chap. 7.

16 Bullock, *Six Months' Residence*, p. 61.

17 Francis de Castelnau, *Expédition dans les parties centrales de l'Amérique du sud, 1843–1847* (Paris, 1851), pp. 28–30.

18 Henri de Saussure, *Voyage aux Antilles et au Mexique, 1854–56* (Geneva, 1993), pp. 95–6.

19 M. A. Brissot, *Voyage au Guazacoalcos, aux Antilles et aux Étas-Unis* (Paris, 1837), p. 117.

20 Maria y Campos, *Imagen*, p. 80.

21 Elisabeth Hardouin-Fugier, *Histoire de la corrida en Europe* (Paris, 2005), pp. 61–5.

22 Richard Twiss, *Travels through Portugal and Spain* (Dublin, 1775).

23 William Dalrymple, *Travels through Spain and Portugal in 1774* (London, 1777).

24 Richard Crocker, *Travels through Several Provinces of Spain and Portugal* (London, 1799).

25 Joseph Townsend, *A Journey through Spain in the Years 1786 and 1787* (London, 1791).

26 William Beckford, The *Journal of William Beckford in Portugal and Spain, 1787–1788* (London, 1954).

27 Jean-François Peyron, *Nouveau voyage en Espagne fait en 1777 et 1778* (London, 1782), vol. I.

28 Henri Swinburne, *Voyage d'Henri Swinburne en Espagne, en 1775 et 1776* (Paris, 1787).

29 Norbert Caimo, *Voyage d'Espagne fait en l'année 1755* (Paris, 1772), vol. I.

30 Joseph Baretti, *A Journey from London to Genoa through England, Portugal, Spain and France* (Sussex, 1970).

31 Peter Löfling, *Reisebeschreibung nach den Spanischen Ländern in Europa und America in den Jahren 1751 bis 1756* (Berlin, 1776).

32 Edward Clarke, *Letters Concerning the Spanish Nation; Written at Madrid during the Years 1760 and 1761* (London, 1763), pp. 107–15.

33 William Beckford, *Italy with Sketches of Spain and Portugal* (Paris, 1834).

34 Beckford, *Journal*, p. 127.

35 Friedrich Link, *Bemerkungen auf einer Reise durch Frankreich, Spanien und vorzüglich Portugal* (Kiel, 1801), pp. 233–5.

36 Baretti, *A Journey from London*, vol. I, pp. 86–90.

37 Fleuriot de Langle, *Voyage de Figaro en Espagne* (Saint-Malo, 1784).

38 Robert Favre, *Voyage de Figaro en Espagne* (Saint-Étienne, 1995).

39 Jean-Luc Guichet, *J. J. Rousseau, L'animal et l'homme* (Paris, 2006), p. 368.

40 Dalrymple, *Travels*, p. 9.

41 Christian August Fischer, *Travels in Spain in the Years 1797 and 1798*, trans. Frederick Augustus Fischer (London, 1802), p. 50.

42 Richard Twiss, in *La Fête espagnole des taureaux*, ed. A. Lafront (Paris, 1988), p. 140.

43 Link, *Bemerkungen*, p. 236.

44 Jacob Volkmann, *Neueste Reisen durch Spanien* (Leipzig, 1785), p. 334.

45 Arthur-William Costignan, *Voyage de Costignan en Portugal* (Paris, 1804), in *La Fête espagnole des taureaux*, ed. A. Laffront (Paris, 1988), p. 182.

46 Beckford, *Journal*, p. 154.

47 Baretti, *A Journey from London*, vol. I, p. 86.

48 Jean-François Bourgoing, *Modern State of Spain* (London, 1808), vol. II, pp. 355–7.

49 Désiré Charnay, *Voyage au Mexique, 1858–1861* (Paris, 2001), p. 192.

five: Nineteenth-century Spain and Latin America

1 Michel Delon, *L'idée d'énergie au tournant des Lumières 1770–1820* (Paris, 1988), pp. 152, 215–22.

2 Charles Baudelaire, *Poems*, trans. Richard Howard (London, 1993), p. 206.

3 Christine Marcandier-Colard, *Crimes de sang et scènes capitales, essai sur l'esthétique romantique de la violence* (Paris, 1998) p. 15.

4 Fabrice Malkani, 'Entre quiétude et inquiétude: l'animal, messager de l'ouvert dans l'oeuvre de Rilke', in *l'Amour des animaux dans le monde germanique* ed. M. Cluet (Rennes, 2004) pp. 253–5.

5 Douglas Gibb, *Childe Harold's Pilgrimage* (Paris, 1922).

6 John A. Dix, *A Winter in Madeira, a Summer in Spain* (New York, 1851), Canto i, 80, p. 267.

7 Thomas Roscoe, *The Tourist in Spain* (London, 1836).

8 *European Traveller Artists, Artists in XIXth-century Mexico* (Palacio Iturbide, Mexico, 1996), in particular P. Diener, p. 137, and Scott Wilcox, pp. 127–34.

9 Bullock, *Six Months' Residence and Travels in Mexico* (London, 1824), p. 61.

10 *Description of a View of a City of Mexico and surrounding Country now exhibiting in the Panorama Leicester Square* (London, 1825); J. R. Burford, *Pamphlet for the Panorama of the City of Mexico exhibited by Bullock.*

11 Wilfried Eberstein, *Das Tierschutzrecht in Deutschland, bis zum Erlass des Reichs-Tierschutzgesetzes vom 24 November 1933* (Frankfurt am Main, 1999), p. 41.

12 Juan Pedro Viqueira Alban, *Relajados o reprimidos, diversiones publicas y vida social* (Mexico, 2003).

13 Nicolas Rangel, *Historia del toreo en Mexico, epoca colonial, 1529–1821* (Mexico, 1924).

14 Jose Rogelio Alvarez, ed., *Enciclopedia de Mexico* (Mexico, 1977).

15 Serge Gruzinski, *Histoire de Mexico* (Paris, 1996), p. 328.

16 Elisabeth Hardouin-Fugier, *Histoire de la corrida en Europe* (Paris, 2005), pp. 98–103.

17 Nigel Glendenning, in *Goya, Das Zeitalter der Revolution, Kunst um 1800*, ed. Werner Hofmann (Hamburg, 1981), p. 289.

18 José Manuel Matilla, *El libro de la Tauromaquia, Francisco de Goya* (Madrid, 2001), in particular, Javier Blas Benito, *Prologo*, pp. 11–13; José Manuel Matilla and José Miguel Medrano, *Vision critica de un fiesta* (Madrid, 2001); José Manuel Matilla, 'Goya y la vision critica de la tauromaquia', *El Pais* (24 March 2008), p. 50.

19 Jeannine Baticle, *Goya, Painter of Terrible Splendor* (New York, 1994), p. 134.

20 Elena Santiago and Juliet Wilson-Bareau, *Goya en la biblioteca nacional* (Madrid, 1996), no. 325.

21 Dix, *A Winter in Madeira*, pp. 265–7.

22 Francisco Montes Reina, *Tauromaquia completa o sea el arte de torear en plaza tanto a pie como a caballo* (Madrid, 1836).

23 Coluche, *Les voyages*, Leaflet, ed. V. Sofronadies 'Ce que vous devez savoir sur une corrida' (1999).

24 Jean Cau, *Réflexions dures sur une époque molle* (Paris, 1981), p. 44.

25 Elias Canetti, *The Human Province*, trans. Joachim Neugroschel (London, 1985), p. 12.

26 George Bernard Shaw, 'Saint Joan', in *The Complete Plays of Bernard Shaw* (London, 1937), p. 1007.

27 Michel Leiris, *Francis Bacon, face et profil* (Paris, 1983), p. 47.

28 Bartolomé Bennassar, *La Tauromachie* (Paris, 2003), pp. 104–6.

29 Fernando Sommer d'Andrade, *La Tauromachie équestre au Portugal* (Paris, 1991), p. 70.

30 Angel Lopez Cantos, *Juegos, fiestas y diversiones en la América espanola* (Madrid, 1992), p. 170.

31 Danièle Demélas, Yves Saint-Geour, *Vie quotidienne en Amérique du sud au temps de Bolivar* (Paris, 1987), p 170.

32 Henri Favre, *Indianité, ethnocide, indigénisme en Amérique latine* (Toulouse, 1982), p. 80.

33 Leonida Rivera, alias Don Maximo, *Charlas de evocacion taurina, la tauromachia en el Peru 1816–1940 y en Espana, Perifoneadas por radio Nacional del Peru* (Lima, 1959).

34 William Bennett Stevenson, *A Historical and Descriptive Narrative of 20 Years' Residence in South America* (London, 1825), vol. II, pp. 307–8.

35 Charles d'Ursel, *Séjours et voyages au Brésil, à La Plata, au Chili, en Bolivie et au Pérou* (Paris, 1880), p. 273.

36 José Maria de Cossio, *Los Toros, Tratado técnico et historico* (Madrid, 1969), vol. IV, p. 190.

37 Paul Marcoy, *Voyage à travers l'Amérique du sud, de l'océan Pacifique à l'Océan Atlantique* (Paris, 1869), p. 306.

six: Bullfighting, Art, Opera and Dance

1 R. W. Hardy, *Travels in the Interior of Mexico in 1825–28* (London, 1829), p. 31.

2 José Maria de Heredia, *Œuvres poétiques complètes* (Paris, 1984), p. 212.

3 Isidore Loewenstern, *La Mexique, souvenir d'un voyageur* (Paris and Leipzig, 1853), pp. 142–3.

4 Manuel Landaeta Rosales, *Los toros en Caracas desde 1560* (Caracas, 1971), p. 8.

5 Ernest Röthlisberger, *Viajeros por Colombia* (Bogota, 1929), p. 129.

6 Maria Justinia Sarabia Viejo, *El juego de Gallos en Nueva España* (Seville, 1972).

7 Charles Blanchot, *Mémoires, intervention française*

au Mexico (Paris, 1911), vol. II, pp. 184–7.

8 Emma D. de Saldaña, *Las Voces del Silencio* (Mexico, 2004) p. 239.

9 Maurice Agulhon, 'Le Sang des Bêtes', *Romantisme* (1981), pp. 104–7.

10 Bartolomé Bennassar, *Histoire de la tauromachie* (Paris, 2002), pp. 21–6.

11 Alvaro Martinez-Novillo, *Le Peintre et la tauromachie*, trans. Louis Audibert (Paris, 1988), p. 121.

12 Mario Bois, *Le Taureau des fêtes* (Paris, 1974), p. 49.

13 Juliet Wilson-Bareau, *Édouard Manet, Voyage en Espagne* (Paris, 1988), p. 23.

14 Robert Bérard, 'Manet', in *La tauromachie*, ed. R. Bérard (Paris, 2003), p. 623.

15 Maria Dolorès Falacios Lopez, *Arte y toros, estampa e ilustracion taurina* (Madrid, 2004), p. 55.

16 Gustave Doré and Charles Davillier, *Voyage en Espagne* (Paris, 1980), p. 87.

17 Philippe Néagu, 'Célestine Galli-Marié', *Nadar* (Paris, 1994), p. 555.

18 Saldaña, *Las voces del silencio*, p.166.

19 Dominique Maingueneau, *Carmen, racines d'un mythe* (Paris, 1984).

20 Adrian Shubert, *Death and Money in the Afternoon* (Oxford, 1999), p. 85.

seven: Beyond Spain

1 Adrian Shubert, *Death and Money in the Afternoon* (Oxford, 1999), p. 117.

2 Ibid., graph 2, p. 219.

3 Raphael Alberti, 'The Lost Grove', in Shubert, *Death*, pp. 165, 217.

4 Robert von Hippel, *Die Tierquälerei in der Strafgesetzgebung des In-und Auslandes* (Berlin, 1891), p. 90.

5 *Bulletin de la Société protectrice des Animaux* (Paris, 1895), pp. 329–32.

6 Shubert, *Death and Money*, pp. 174–80.

7 Michel Porcheron, 'Las Corrida de toros en Cuba, esquisse de l'histoire d'un échec', in *Tauromachies en Amérique latine*, ed. J. Ortiz (Anglet, 2004), pp. 109–41.

8 Santiago Esteras Gil, *Leccion antitaurina* (Alicante, 1974), p. 146; Emma D. de Saldaña, *Las Voces del Silencio* (Mexico, 2001), p. 277.

9 José Emilio A. Calmell, *Relato Historico de la plaza de toros de Lima* (Lima, 1936), p. 46. L. Rivera,

Charlas de evocación taurina: La tauromaquia en el Peru (1816–1940) y en España (Lima, 1959), pp. 35–6. Francisco Lopez-Izquierdo, *Los Toros del nuevo mundo (1942–1992)* (Madrid, 1992), p. 248.

10 Camille Pradier-Fodéré, *Lima et ses environs, Tableaux de mœurs péruviennes* (Paris, 1897), pp. 280–85.

11 Manuel A. Fuentes, *Lima, or Sketches of the Capital of Peru, Historical, Statistical, Administrative, Commercial and Moral* (London, 1866), p. 141.

12 Max Radiguet, *Souvenirs de l'Amérique espagnole* (Paris, 1856).

13 Jean-Michel Lemogodeuc, 'Taureaux et corridas au Vénézuela', *La Corrida en Amérique du Sud*, ed. Ortiz, p. 79–86.

14 Carlo Salas, *Los Toros en Vénézuéla* (Caracas, 1981), p. 23.

15 Pierre Dupuy, 'Élevages mexicains' in *Toros* (25 November 1997).

16 Augustin Linarès, *Toreros mexicanos* (Mexico, 1958).

17 J. B. Trouplin, 'Gaona y Jiménez, Rodolfo', in *La Tauromachie*, ed. R. Bérard (Paris, 2003), p. 508.

18 Shubert, *Death and Money*, pp. 90–91.

19 Lopez-Izquierdo, *Los toros*, pp. 138, 116, 140, 175, 308.

20 Elisabeth Hardouin-Fugier, *Histoire de la corrida en Europe* (Paris, 2005), pp. 125–48.

21 Elisabeth Hardouin-Fugier, 'La Lente Conquête du jus animalium en Europe', in *Le Bien-être animal*, ed. Conseil de l'Europe (Strasbourg, 2006), p. 189.

22 E. Bersot, 'Le sang des bêtes' (1882); Maurice Agulhon, *Romantisme* (1981), p. 107.

23 Eric Baratay and Elisabeth Hardouin-Fugier, *La Corrida* (Paris, 1995), pp. 47–8.

24 Henri de Montherlant, 'Pas de Corridas dans les régions de France où elles n'ont que faire!', *L'Auto* (9 February 1933).

25 Michael A. Ogorzaly, *When Bulls Cry* (Bloomington, IN, 2006), p. 53.

26 Claude Popelin, *Le Taureau et son combat* (Paris, 1981), p. 81.

27 Robert Zaretsky, *Le Coq et le taureau; comment le marquis de Baroncelli a inventé la Camargue* (Marseille, 2007), pp. 17 etc.

28 Auguste Lafront, *Histoire de la corrida en France* (Paris, 1977), pp. 86–9.

29 *Délibérations du Conseil Municipal*, 3 August 1901, Nîmes, Municipal Archives, R. 287, R 288.

30 Baratay and Hardouin-Fugier *La Corrida*, pp. 47–8.

31 Octave Mirbeau, 'De la pierre à la bête' *Le Journal* (17 June 1900), in *Chroniques taurines de Louis Feuillade*, ed. B. Bastide (Nîmes, 1998) p. 33.

32 Paul Couturiau, *Séverine l'insurgée*, (Paris, 2001).

33 Frédéric Ozanam, *Lettres de F. Ozanam, les dernières années* (Paris, 1992), Ozanam to Charles, Biarritz, 17 September 1852, p. 386.

34 Frédéric Ozanam, 'Une pélerinage au pays du Cid,' *Le Correspondant* (25 October 1853), pp. 8–55.

35 *Bulletin de l'Œuvre d'Assistance aux Bêtes d'Abattoir* (Paris, 1986–7), p. 53.

eight: The Influence of Art, Film and History

1 Jean Bescos, *Affiches de corrida* (Paris, 1996).

2 Michael A. Ogorzaly, *When Bulls Cry* (Bloomington, IN, 2006), pp. 68–73.

3 Vaslav Nijinsky, *The Diary of Vaslav Nijinsky*, trans. Romola Nijinksy (London, 1991) p. 29.

4 Sergei Eisenstein, *Dessins secrets*, ed. Jean Claude Marcadé and A. Ackerman (Paris 1999).

5 Sergei Eisenstein, *¡Que Viva Mexico!*, 1931–2, III Fiesta, G. Alexandrov, Mexican Picture Trust, Upton Sinclair, California.

6 Robert Bérard, 'Manolete', *La Tauromachie*, ed. R. Bérard (Paris, 2003), pp. 81–7.

7 Henri de Montherlant, *The Matador*, trans. Peter Wiles (London, 1957) pp. 57, 44.

8 Henri de Montherlant, 'Pas de corrida dans les régions de France où elles n'ont que faire!', *l'Auto* (9 February 1933).

9 Nathalie Barberger, *Michel Leiris, l'écriture du deuil* (Strasbourg, 1998), p. 178.

10 François Zumbiehl, *Des Taureaux dans la tête* (Paris, 2004), p. 32.

11 Georges Bataille, *Story of the Eye*, trans. Joachim Neugroschel (Harmondsworth, 1979), p. 47.

12 Michel Leiris, *Le Miroir de la tauromachie* (Paris, 1981).

13 Michel Surya, *Georges Bataille, an Intellectual Biography*, trans. Krzysztof Fijalkowski and Michael Richardson (London, 2002), p. 119.

14 Marcel Mauss, 'Essai sur la nature et la fonction du sacrifice, 1899', in M. Mauss, *Œuvre complet de Marcel Mauss* (Paris, 1968), p. 301.

15 Louis Vincent Thomas, *Anthropologie de la Mort* (Paris, 1976), p. 98.

16 Michel Leiris, *Scraps*, trans. Lydia Davis (Baltimore, 1997), p. 39.

17 Ibid., p. 123.

18 Michel Cournot, 'Leiris le matador', *Le Nouvel Observateur* (18–24 July 2002), pp. 80–81.

19 Francis Marmande, Preface to *La Course de taureaux*, *Michael Leiris* (Paris 1991), pp. 13–14.

20 Timothy Mitchell and Rosaria Cambria, *Blood Sport, a Social History of Spanish Bullfighting* (Philadelphia, 1991), pp. 16, 41.

21 Julian Pitt-Rivers, *Le Temps de la réflexion* (Paris, 1983) p. 189.

22 Francis Wolff, 'Qui est le taureau?' in *Des taureaux et des hommes*, ed. A. Molinié (Paris, 1999), p. 28.

23 Jérôme Forsans, *Toros* (29 March 2001), p. 2.

24 Julian Pitt-Rivers, 'La Estructura trinitaria del Sacrificio', in *La Tauromaquia considerada como un 'sacrifice'*, ed. Pedro Romero de Solis (Seville, 1995), pp. 46–57, 198.

25 Ogorzaly, *When Bulls Cry*, pp. 62–3.

26 José María Arguedas, *Yawar Fiesta* (Paris, 2002).

27 Yves Harté, 'Yawar Fiesta', in *Tauromachies en Amérique latine*, ed. Jean Ortiz (Anglet, 2004), pp. 143–7.

28 Mario Vargas Llosa, *L'Utopie archaïque* (Paris, 1996), p. 162.

29 Fernando Ponce Matamoros, *La Pensée Coloniale, Découverte, conquête et guerre des dieux au Mexique* (Paris, 2002).

30 Emma de Saldaña, *Las Voces del silencio* (Mexico, 2001), p. 132.

31 Surya, *Georges Bataille*, p. 98.

32 Bataille, *Story of the Eye*, trans. Neugroschel, pp. 47–54 (parenthetical page numbers refer to this edition).

33 Maurice Heine, *Le Marquis de Sade*, Preface by Gilbert Lely (Paris, 1950).

34 Georges Bataille, *L'Erotisme* (Paris, 1957), p. 216.

35 Jean Cocteau, *La Corrida du 1° Mai* (Paris, 1957), p. 90.

36 Georges Bataille, *La Littérature et le mal* (Paris, 1957), p. 121.

37 Georges Bataille, *Theory of Religion*, trans. Robert Hurley (New York, 1989), p. 22.

nine: In the Twentieth Century

1 *Anuario taurino, 1937–1938, resumen estadistico* (Mexico, 1938).

2 D. Bessières, 'Mexico et ses tor-héros', in *La*

Corrida en Amérique ed. J. Ortiz (Anglet, 2004), pp. 47–53.

3 Luis de Tabique, *Guia de America Taurina* (Mexico, 1955).

4 José Luis Lopez, *El Financiero* (18 January 1996), in Emma D. de Saldaña, *Las Voces del silencio* (Mexico, 2004), pp. 209–10.

5 Manolillo, *Toros* (January 2005, 5 August 2001, 16 March 2007).

6 Saldaña, *Las Voces*, p. 165.

7 Tabique, *Guia*, p. 302.

8 Claude Bouet, 'Élevages mexicains', *Toros* (18 January 1991), p. 10; (28 January 1991), pp. 20–32.

9 Saldaña, *Las Voces*, p. 211.

10 Jean Cau, *Fernando Botero, Corrida* (Paris, 1990), pp. 146–7.

11 Elias Canetti, *Crowds and Power*, trans. Carol Stewart (London, 2000), p. 176.

12 Caballero-Bonald, *Botero* (Paris, 1989); *L'oreille*, p. 179.

13 Cau, *Fernando Botero*, p. 146.

14 Kenneth Lynn, *Hemingway* (London, 1987), pp. 38–48.

15 Ernest Hemingway, *For Whom the Bell Tolls*, quoted in *Hemingway's Spain* (San Francisco, CA, 1989), p. 19.

16 Jose Luis Castillo Puche, *Hemingway in Spain* (New York, 1974).

17 Ernest Hemingway, *Death in the Afternoon* (London, 2000), p. 2.

18 John Malcolm Brinnin, *The Third Rose: Gertrude Stein and her World* (Boston, 1959), quoted in Ogorzaly, *When Bulls Cry*, p. 100.

19 Rafael Abella, *La vida cotidiana a l'Espana republicana* (Barcelona, 1975), p. 97.

20 *La Vie culturelle sous l'occupation, la documentation française* (Paris, 1939–45), no. 38, 40–41.

21 Jean Lacouture, *Signes du Taureau* (Paris, 1979), p. 138.

22 Ogorzaly, *When Bulls Cry*, p. 73.

23 Lynn, *Hemingway*, p. 397.

24 Hemingway, *Death in the Afternoon*, p. 87.

25 Ibid., p. 363.

26 Ogorzaly, *When Bulls Cry*, pp. 55–85.

27 Rico Godoy, *Diario 16*; Saldaña, *Las Voces*, p. 226.

28 Jules Supervielle, *L'Étoile de Séville* (Paris, 1957), p. 181.

29 A. Dubos, 'Edito, mort d'afición', *Tendido*, no. 45 (January 1991).

30 Philippe Dagen, *Francis Bacon* (Paris, 1996), p. 94, quoting Deleuze, *Francis Bacon, logique de la sensation* (Paris, 1981).

31 David Sylvester, *Interviews with Francis Bacon, 1962–1979* (London, 1975), p. 48.

32 Elisabeth Hardouin-Fugier, *Histoire de la corrida en Europe* (Paris, 2005), pp. 194–208.

33 Pierre Braunberger, filmmaker, *La Course de taureaux, images animées*, Auguste Lafront, scriptwriter, Michel Leiris, Jean Desailly, Paris, Panthéon Production, *Les Films du jeudi* distributors, 1951, 1993, 2005.

34 Julian Pereda, *Los Toros ante la Iglesia y la Moral* (Madrid, 1945).

35 Jean-Louis Lopez, 'L'église aujourd'hui', *Corrida*, no. 8 (November 1981), p. 29.

36 José Delgado, alias Pepe-Hillo, *La tauromaquia o arte de torear*, ed. Gustavo Gili (Barcelona, 1958).

37 Pablo Picasso and Luis-Miguel Dominguín, *Toros y toreros*, 3rd edn (Paris, 1993).

ten: Modern Times

1 Hélène Peroz, 'La Tradition tauromachique et le droit pénal français', in *Des Toros et des hommes*, ed. A. Molinié (Paris, 1999), pp. 249–56.

2 Eric Baratay and Elisabeth Hardouin-Fugier, *La Corrida* (Paris, 1995), p. 52.

3 Order of non-suit, 19 December 2001, Pau Court of Appeal, *Le Pavé dans l'arène*, Fédération des Luttes Anti-Corrida, no. 19, 4° Trimestre 2001, p. 17.

4 Ernest Hemingway, *Death in the Afternoon* (London, 2000), p. 72.

5 *Le Figaro* (3 August 2000).

6 Marc Roumengou, *Dossier Manolete* (Mirepoix-sur-Tarn, 1999).

7 *Toros* (8 June 2007).

8 Antonio Moreno, Malaga, Àlvaro Mùnera, *Le procès de la corrida en Espagne, en France et au Portugal*, Franz Weber Foundation, 23 June 2008.

9 'Debt in the Afternoon', *The Guardian* (12 May 2008).

10 Robert Bérard, 'Statistiques 2001', in *La Tauromachie*, ed. R. Bérard (Paris, 2003), p. 1008.

11 Dominique Dubois, President of the ECTPR in South-East France

12 Jean-Claude Roux, *Toros* (6 April 2007); Claude Mauron, 'Toros en France', *Toros* (8 April 2005).

13 Antonio Lorca, *El Pais* (8 April 2008).

14 Pierre Daulouède, *Toromania* (Pau, 2003), pp. 89, 103.
15 Ibid., pp. 109–10.
16 Marc Lavie, *Corridas en France* (Pau, 2004), pp. 7–8.
17 'El Mundo del toro defendera la Fiesta en el Parlamento Europeo', *ABC* (22 February 2008).
18 *El Pais* (16 December 2006).
19 Los Verdes (1 November 2007), radio programme.
20 'Rapport public, novembre 1997', *Le Journal Officiel* (Paris, 1997), pp. 408–11.
21 Alliance pour la Suppression des Corridas, Nîmes (ASAC).
22 Website of Tolosa Toros, Le Conseil d'administration au maire de Fenouillet, Summer 2005.
23 Hemingway, *Death in the Afternoon*, p. 72.
24 Giorgio Monticelli, *La Tradition tauromachique en Italie* (Paris, 1986), p. 140.
25 Anima Naturalis, *Coordination générale du Front Anti-taurin du Pérou*, 1 October 2007, 'Lima rechaza las corridas de toros'.

eleven: The Fight against Bullfighting Today

1 Elias Canetti, *Crowds and Power*, trans. Carol Stewart (London, 2000), p. 28.
2 Jean Baudrillard, *Symbolic Exchange and Death*, trans. Iain Hamilton Grant (London, 1993), p. 164.
3 Antoine de Latour, *L'Espagne religieuse et littéraire* (Paris, 1863), p. 288.
4 St Augustine, *Confessions*, trans. Henry Chadwick (New York, 1998), p. 101.
5 Matilda Mench, *Life on the Line, the Heroic Story of Vicki Moore* (Liverpool, 2007), p. 129 (Jill Phipps); pp. 134, 181–2.
6 Lucien Scubla, 'Ceci n'est pas une meurtre', in *De la Violence*, ed. Françoise Héritier (Paris, 1999), vol. II, p. 148.
7 Pierre Paris, *L'Espagne de 1895 et 1897, journal de voyage* (Alicante, 1979), pp. 102–3.
8 Ernest Hemingway, *Death in the Afternoon* (London, 2000), pp. 5–6.
9 Spain, Torrelavaga, Cantabria, August 2005.
10 Henri Bergson, *Laughter, an Essay on the Meaning of the Comic*, trans. Cloudesley Brereton and Fred Rothwell (London, 1911), p. 4.
11 *Toros* (25 December 2008).
12 Bernard Lempert, *Critique de la pensée sacrificielle* (Paris, 2000), p. 60.
13 Jean-Paul Sartre, *Witness to my Life: The Letters of Jean-Paul Sartre to Simone de Beauvoir* trans. Lee Fahnestock and Norman MacAfee (London, 1992), p. 208.
14 Franquin, *Fluide glacial* (Paris, 2007), p. 57.
15 Luis G. Soto, *Paz, guerra y violencia* (Acoruna, 2006), p. 97.
16 Pierre Molas, *Parler toro* (Pau, 2000), p. 52.
17 Jordi Casamitjana '"Suffering" in Bullfighting Bulls; An "ethologist perspective"', *Le procès de la corrida en Espagne, en France et au Portugal*, ed. Franz Weber Geneva, 23 June 2008.
18 Oyola, Fabiano Andrés, *Toros y bueyes, La tradicion ganadera y taurina de la dehesa* (Badajoz, 2008), p. 168.
19 http://lesactualitesdudroit.20minutes-blogs.fr, 1 September 2008.
20 Yves Cochet, *Question publiée au Journal Officiel*, 29 January 2008, p. 698, reply: 11 March 2008, p. 2133.
21 Elisabeth de Fontenay, 'Apologie de la corrida, retour sur une maltraitance festive', *Libération des Philosophes*, 8 November 2007, p. 33. Demande d'interdiction des enfants aux arènes, 30 January 2008, handwritten, letter to Elisabeth Hardouin-Fugier.
22 Pierre Matté, *Blessure et mort du taureau de combat, étude anatomico-pathologique* (Toulouse, 1929), Autopsies, Nîmes Bullring, 25 July 1926, p. 71.
23 Hemingway, *Death in the Afternoon*, pp. 50–51.
24 Christophe Chay, *La Tauromachie* (Paris, 2003), pp. 287–9.
25 Miguel Darrieumerlou, *Toros* (September 2006), p. 31.
26 Jean Decety, 'Comment notre cerveau perçoit la douleur d'autrui', in *Homme et animal: de la douleur à la cruauté*, ed. T. Auffret van der Kemp and J. C. Nouët (Paris, 2008), p. 154.
27 Joël Lequesne, 'Procès de la corrida: le point de vue d'un psychologue de l'éducation', Fondation Franz Weber, Geneva, 23 June 2008. Jean-Paul Richier, Rencontres Animal et Société, Ministry of Agriculture, May 2008.
28 *Catechism of the Catholic Church* (Paris, 1992), no. 2417.
29 Roland Minnerath, *Letter to J. C. Nouët*, Paris, 28–29 October 2004.
30 Andrew Linzey, 'Animal rights', *Dictionary of Ethics, Theology and Society* (London, 1996), pp. 29–31.

31 Andrew Linzey, *Christianity and the Rights of Animals* (New York, 1987), pp. 108–10.

32 Isaiah 1:11, King James Bible.

33 Jean Grondin, 'Derrida et la question animale', *Cités*, 30 (2007), p. 36.

34 Paul Virilio to Béatriz MacDowell, 27 May 2007.

35 Marta Tafalla, *Los Derechos de los animales* (Madrid, 2004), pp. 239–48.

36 Michael A. Ogorzaly, *When Bulls Cry* (Bloomington, IN, 2006), p. 104.

37 François Cavanna, *Coups de sang* (Paris, 1991), p. 14.

38 Luce Lapin, 'L'Agonie du taureau marron: la corrida, c'est ça!', *Charlie Hebdo* (15 June 2005), Puces 678, p. 14.

39 Ogorzaly, *When Bulls Cry*, pp. 133–45.

40 *Routard Guide*, Mexico (Paris, 2003), p. 72.

41 Manolillo, editor, *Toros* (16 March 2007).

42 www.liberation.fr, 30 January 2007.

43 Manuel Vicent, 'Mas Toros', *El Pais* (7 May 2006).

44 Saldaña, *Las Voces*, p. 46.

45 Fondation Altarriba, Amigos de los Animales, International Court for Animal Rights, Franz Weber, Geneva, 23 June 2008.

Photo Acknowledgements

The author and publishers wish to express their thanks to the below sources of illustrative material and/or permission to reproduce it. (Some information not placed in the captions for reasons of brevity is also given below.)

Images © ADAGP, Paris and DACS, London 2009: p. 14 (foot), p. 47 (right), 98 (top), 138, 140, 181; The Josef and Anni Albers Foundation, Bethany, CT (© The Josef and Anni Albers Foundation/VG Bild-Kunst, Bonn and DACS, London 2009): p. 6; Art Institute of Chicago: p. 104 (top); artwork by author: p. 30; photo by author: p. 169 (top); © The Estate of Francis Bacon – all rights reserved – DACS 2009: p. 161; photo courtesy of the Biblothèque Municipale, Lyon: p. 50 (foot); Bibliothèque Nationale de France, Paris: pp. 65, 78, 107; British Museum, London: 79; British Museum, London (Department of Prints and Drawings): pp. 16, 62, 81, 86, 109, 150; photos © The Trustees of the British Museum: pp. 16, 18, 21 (foot), 62, 79, 86, 89, 109, 150; photo © CAP / Roger-Viollet: p. 120; photos © CAS International (Comité Anti Stierenvechten): pp. 26, 32, 168, 171, 185; courtesy of CAS International: pp. 26, 28, 29, 32, 56, 58, 142, 169 (foot), 171, 185, 189; reproduced courtesy of the artist (Sergui Chepnik): p. 43; © DACS 2009: pp. 27, 41, 50 (foot); Dalí Museum, Figueras: p. 146; Salvador Dalí Museum, St Petersburg, Florida: p. 130 (foot); from Jean-Charles Davillier, *Le Voyage en Espagne* (Paris, 1860): p. 105; photos EHF: pp. 24, 60, 91 (foot); courtesy of EXPRMNTL galerie, Toulouse: p. 178; J. Paul Getty Museum at the Getty Center, Los Angeles: p. 85 (foot); photos © Sabine Joosten: pp. 56, 189; courtesy Pablo Knudsen, from his 2007 film *Apprendre à tuer*: p. 182; courtesy of Marius Kolff: p. 170; photos © League Against Cruel Sports (LACS): pp. 28, 29, 58; from Michel Leiris, *Miroir de la Tauromachie* (Paris, 1938): p. 140; courtesy the artist (Zoe Leonard): p. 35; courtesy Jérôme Lescure: p. 42; from the Jérôme Lescure film *Je Possède*: p. 184; Library of Congress, Washington, DC (Prints and Photographs Division): pp. 54 (foot), 57, 72, 74, 118, 151 top (George Grantham Bain Collection), 151 foot (Caroline and Erwin Swann Collection of Caricature and Cartoon); photo Enrique Meneses/Rex Features: p. 157 (top); Metropolitan Museum of Art, New York: pp. 14 (top right), 100 (top); Musée de l'Art Moderne, Paris: pp. 138, 153; Musée des Beaux-Arts, Lyon: p. 161; Musée Bonnat, Bayonne: p. 128; Musée du Louvre, Paris (Cabinet des Dessins): p. 63; Musée des Modernes, Antwerp: p. 98 (foot); Musée d'Orsay, Paris: p. 101; Museo del Prado, Madrid: pp. 8, 66, 69, 82, 83 (foot); Museo de la Real Academia de Bellas Artes de San Fernando, Madrid: p. 14 (top left); Museo de la Reina, Sofia: p. 50 (foot); Museo Municipal, Madrid: p. 10; National Gallery of Art, Washington, DC: pp. 99, 125; photo Tim Nighswander: p. 6; The Phillips Collection, Washington, DC: p. 100 (foot); private collections: p. 14 (foot), 27, 39, 135, 154; courtesy Professeur François Robichon: p. 137; reproduced courtesy of the artist (Tony Quimbel): p. 44; © Salvador Dalí, Gala-Salvador Dalí Foundation, DACS, London 2009: p. 130 (foot), 146; courtesy of José Luis Grosson Seran: p. 183; © SHARK (SHowing Animals Respect and Kindness): p. 142; from Théodore Simons, *L'Espagne* (Paris, 1884): p. 45; © Succession Picasso/DACS 2009: pp. 135, 154; photo TS/Keystone USA/Rex Features: p. 157 (foot); from José Velazquez y Sanchez, *Anales del Toreo* (Seville, 1868): p. 91 (top); from Charles Wiener, *Pérou et Bolivie, récit de voyage . . .* (Paris, 1880): p. 52; photo Ghislain Zucolo: p. 159.

Index

Numbers in *italics* refer to page numbers of illustrations.